FamilyCircle®

KiDS PARTY bOOK

CONFIDENT COOKING

The Family Circle Promise of Success

Welcome to the world of Confident Cooking,
created for you in the **Family Circle Test Kitchen**,
where recipes are double-tested by
our team of home economists to achieve a
high standard of success – and delicious
results every time.

MURDOCH BOOKS®

Sydney • London • Vancouver • New York

CONT

PLANNING a PARTY

4 — 7

Advice on how to organise the party in advance, and what to do on the day.

PARTY THEMES

8 —17

Twenty theme packages, including suggestions for decorations and invitations, cakes and games.

CAKE recipes

18 — 19

Recipes for the basic cakes and icings needed for all party cakes.

PARTY CAKES

20 — 41

Instructions for creating and decorating number cakes and theme-related cakes.

PARTY FOOD

42 — 65

Crowd-pleasing food ranging from sweet and savoury snacks to sit-down meals.

FRONT COVER: **top left**, *Fairy Wand Biscuit (recipe page 42)*, **below** *(left to right)*, *party sweets, Psychedelic Fairy Bread (recipe page 42), Snowman (recipe page 55) and Pirate Face Biscuits (recipe page 47). Illustration of party invitation by John Yates.*

E n T S

PARTY DrinKS

66 — 69

Thirst-quenching refreshments for totally cool kids.

Take-Home TReaTS

70 — 79

Imaginative suggestions for filling and packaging take-home bags.

PARTY GAmes

80 — 99

Games to please kids of different interests, abilities and age groups.

cake TEMPLATES

100 — 109

Cake shapes drawn to scale and ready for hand-copying or the photocopier.

InDeX

110 — 111

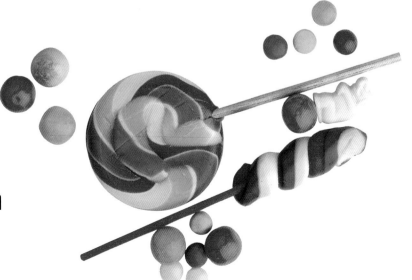

USEFUL inFORmaTion

112

PLANNING a PARTY

CHILDREN'S PARTIES CAN be small, informal events or big productions—as organiser it's up to you to decide how much you can take on. Using a theme for a party can make your job a lot easier, giving the party focus and making it memorable for a long time afterwards.

THE PLANNING

A FEW WEEKS before the party, sit down with your child and work out the basics.

■ If you are having one, choose a theme for the party (pages 8 to 17 will help you). Decide whether you want children to attend in fancy dress or whether you will provide costumes or partial costumes at the party (eg. pirate hats or clown face-painting).

▲ Decide how many children to invite (some families use this rule of thumb—four guests for a four-year-old's party, five for a five-year-old's, and so on). Your child will probably want to invite the whole school, but you are the one with the final say.

● Decide where the party will be held—whether at home, in the local park, or at some special venue appropriate to the party's theme, such as the zoo or the beach. If you are holding the party outside, make sure you have a fall-back plan in case of rain.

◆ Decide when and for how long the party will be held. Parents will need to know when to pick their children up, and you will need to know when you can expect a rest. Don't be too ambitious here—three hours is maximum.

■ Establish the main foods and drinks you will serve—will there just be a table of nibbles, or a full sit-down meal? Are particular foods appropriate to the theme you've chosen? What kind of birthday cake will you provide? Each party plan in this book has food and drink and cake suggestions.

▲ List the games you will have at the party. Organised games are a good way to keep the group in harmony and to channel the energy the children will bring to the party. See pages 80 to 99 for many party games, and pages 8 to 17 for games appropriate to the party themes.

● Work out the format of the party. In what order are you going to have the gift-giving, food and drink, birthday cake, games? Make sure you include some time for free play—sometimes the best fun children have at a party is the fun they make themselves.

All of these things, and all your decisions about decorations, invitations and costumes, will depend on two things: your energy level and your budget. Remember that often the simplest parties are the most successful, because the hosts are relaxed enough to set a happy tone. If your budget is limited, for example, don't be afraid to break with tradition and choose non-competitive group games, such as Follow-the-Leader or Blowing Bubbles, for which no prizes are awarded.

All this planning should result in two lists: 'Things to Buy' and 'Things to Do'. Divide the shopping list into perishables and other items that can be purchased ahead of time. Divide the cooking up in a similar way. Work out a schedule of all the things you and your helpers must do before the party, put it up in a prominent place and make sure you keep to it to avoid a last-minute panic.

Spending a little time organising the party will be rewarded on the day

Involve your children as much as possible in the organisation—they will consider even supermarket shopping to be fun when you are buying things for the party. You can make the invitations together, with the child illustrating and you writing them. Older children can organise their own costumes, but younger children will really appreciate your help.

Establish early on what other help you can rely on. If you know the parents of some of your guests quite well, you might ask them to bring along some of the food or help with the preparations on the day. If you have (or know) older children who would like to earn extra pocket money, delegate games organising, music monitoring or cleaning up after the party to them. As a rule of thumb, do the things you know you are good at and can cope with, and get assistance with the rest.

THE TIMING

IF YOUR CHILD'S birthday happens to fall in the most busy working weeks of the year, such as Christmas, consider holding the party at a quieter time, before or after the rush, with only a small family celebration on the actual day.

Similarly, the day of the week and the time of day should be carefully chosen. If your budget is limited, you may wish to have a morning-tea or afternoon-tea party, rather than providing a full meal. If you are planning a large or very fancy party for example give yourself at least a full day to get

ready by holding the party on a Sunday afternoon. A party for younger children might be best held in the morning or at lunch-time so that they are not too tired before they begin. For children who all attend the same school, a Friday afternoon party, with you collecting the children from school and their parents picking them up a few hours later can be very convenient all round—it leaves your weekend free and allows guests' parents to wind down their working week gently.

THE INVITATIONS

SEND OR GIVE out invitations about two weeks before the party date, and include the following information:

■ whose party it is, and for what occasion (so that guests will know whether to bring a gift);
▲ the date and time of the party, including pick-up time;
● the address of the party, including a map or any special directions if it's difficult to find or to park nearby. It's a good idea to include your phone number, as well; and
◆ any special information: Do you want parents to attend too? Are guests to come in fancy dress? Will the venue change if there is rain, and, if so, to where?

Pages 8 to 17 contain ideas for making your own theme-related invitations. The birthday boy or girl will enjoy helping here. You can also find ready-made invitations in newsagencies or supermarkets.

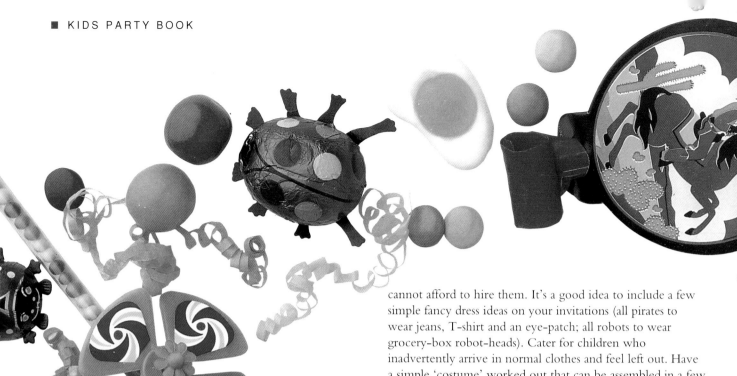

THE **DECORATIONS**

SOMETIMES THE BEST fun of a party is working out how to give your home or party venue an appropriate atmosphere. This can be done quite simply with a bunch of balloons and some coloured streamers, or a banner with HAPPY BIRTHDAY! hung up on one wall.

If you are having a theme party, you can put up similar simple decorations, in colours appropriate to the theme—black for a Halloween party, or blue and green for an Underwater party. All the party plans in this book have suggestions for low-cost theme-related decorations, which you can adapt to suit your venue, expertise and budget.

If space is limited, you may need to organise to store some of your furniture elsewhere to make room for dancing or indoor games.

A word about balloons: plenty! Bunches of balloons signal where a party is happening, and contribute to the party atmosphere in a simple and inexpensive way. Children will enjoy playing with (or popping) balloons. (Make sure there are plenty of spares for the ones that burst.) Very young children are likely to be startled and may need comforting if a balloon bursts. Clear away pieces of burst balloon immediately, as they present a choking hazard. If balloons make *you* nervous, put the bunches up high and only give out balloons as the children are leaving.

THEMES AND **FANCY** DRESS

DON'T BE TOO ambitious when choosing a theme, especially if you are asking guests to come in fancy dress. Remember that many people cannot sew costumes, and cannot afford to hire them. It's a good idea to include a few simple fancy dress ideas on your invitations (all pirates to wear jeans, T-shirt and an eye-patch; all robots to wear grocery-box robot-heads). Cater for children who inadvertently arrive in normal clothes and feel left out. Have a simple 'costume' worked out that can be assembled in a few minutes. Crepe paper can be used in some way for almost any theme, and does not have to be sewn, and coloured felt can be cut into shapes and taped onto existing clothes.

As an alternative to full fancy dress, you can provide a partial costume for every guest in the form of a theme-related party hat or mask, for example a black crepe paper vampire cloak, a fairy wand or a Swinging Sixties hippie headband made from plaited multi-coloured wool. Guests can then come in their favourite party clothes, and be dressed up for the theme when they arrive.

FOOD AND **DRINK**

HOW FANCY THE party food is will depend on the duration and timing of the party—will it be held in the afternoon and only include a cake and a few snacks, or will it incorporate a full meal at some stage?

When planning the food and drink, check with your guests' parents in case their child has any allergies to foods such as gluten or dairy products, or is vegetarian. Apart from being simple good manners, this is also a good way to avoid problems on the day. Some children can become quite aggressive or over-active if they eat too many sweet things, and all children are susceptible to over-indulgence, so limit the sweet treats to reasonable quantities. Most children will expect some kind of 'treat' food at parties, but there is no need to put out mountains of sugar. You may decide to offer healthier alternatives, such as sultanas, other dried fruit (especially banana chips) and unsalted nuts (for children over five years of age), and put off producing the sweets until the end of the party—with the cake, or as take-home treats.

If you choose to have a party somewhere other than at your home (for example, a Teddy Bears' Picnic in the park), you will have to choose food that can be transported easily. Think about, for example, how you will get a large, iced cake to the party without damaging it, and how you will keep things cold.

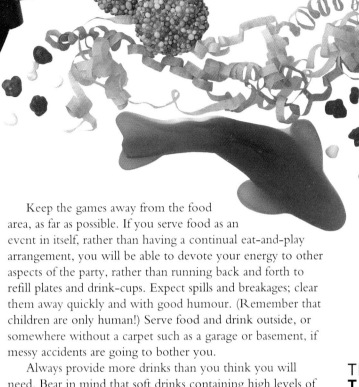

Keep the games away from the food area, as far as possible. If you serve food as an event in itself, rather than having a continual eat-and-play arrangement, you will be able to devote your energy to other aspects of the party, rather than running back and forth to refill plates and drink-cups. Expect spills and breakages; clear them away quickly and with good humour. (Remember that children are only human!) Serve food and drink outside, or somewhere without a carpet such as a garage or basement, if messy accidents are going to bother you.

Always provide more drinks than you think you will need. Bear in mind that soft drinks containing high levels of sugar will make children thirstier—homemade fruit drinks, cordials, milk drinks and plain water are better thirst-quenchers, and won't rev the children up so much.

THE **GAMES**

CHOOSE GAMES THAT are appropriate to the age and abilities of your guests—if you know that some of the children, for example, have problems with reading and writing, avoid games that rely on skill and speed in these areas. Also, some children, especially younger ones, are simply uncompetitive or intimidated by games, so choose at least one or two games that do not require the children to compete against each other. Team games are fine for older children, and are good ice-breakers if the children don't know each other, but make sure that all the children are included regardless of skills or popularity. (It might be best for you to choose the teams, rather than have the children do so.) If numbers are uneven, make sure that every child takes his or her turn sitting out.

Have a varied list of games to keep up the children's interest. Be flexible, so that if a boisterous game looks like getting out of hand you can move to a quieter game. If one game seems to be particularly popular, let it run on, perhaps dropping one of the others you planned.

Don't let the games session drag on. Three or four games (with two or three in reserve) is probably enough. Ten minutes is about as long as any one game will hold the children's interest.

THE **PRIZES** AND **TAKE**-HOME **TREATS**

Decide ahead of time whether you are going to work the games so that every child wins a prize, or whether you will award prizes on the basis of merit—some younger children feel that the latter isn't fair and may become upset if they miss out on a prize. (There is usually one child at every party who can't seem to win anything; if this occurs, play a game in which you can control who wins, such as when-the-music-stops games.) Prizes needn't be expensive, but are more fun if appropriate to the theme of the party.

Take-home treats can be organised ahead of time if you choose fairly non-perishable items. Do not give out the take-home treats until the children are leaving—put a note to yourself on the back of the door as a reminder. It is also a nice idea to send each guest home with a slice of the birthday cake, if there is any left.

Finally, remember that the best planning in the world won't cover all contingencies, so keep a flexible frame of mind. As long as you stay cheerful and relaxed, your guests will take their cue from you. If you are prepared to enjoy yourself, everyone will have fun!

A NOTE ABOUT SAFETY
Remove toothpicks from food before serving to children under five. Do not serve nuts or small sweets to children under five. Supervise games closely and remove any pieces of burst balloon.

PARTY THEMES

FAIRIES

■ **DECORATIONS:** Anything that glitters or looks 'magic', from a sprinkling of glittery cardboard stars around the walls of one room to a complete fairy grotto with the walls draped in metallic-threaded fabric and magic toadstools (cushions slip-covered in white-dotted red fabric) for children to sit on. Drape the table in muslin, tie at the corners with bows, attach glitter-glue stars to light it up here and there.

■ **CAKE:** Pretty Star

■ **FOOD:** Psychedelic Fairy Bread, Fairy Cakes, Fairy Wands, Chicken Toasts, Cheese and Bacon Tarts, Toadstools

■ **DRINK:** Peach Dream

■ **GAMES:** Making Words, Wand Relay, Necklace Race, Ring a Roses

■ **PRIZES:** Simple magic tricks, small hardcover notebooks painted silver and decorated with glitter, plastic jewels.

Please come to a fairy party for .... on .... at .... RSVP ....

OUTER SPACE

■ **DECORATIONS:** Glow-in-the-dark stars and planets can be used on the walls and ceiling; if resources are limited, you can create a black cardboard 'window' out of your 'spaceship' and just cover that. You can create a hi-tech look by putting up cardboard control panels on anything your guests are likely to use, from a row of switches taped to the table beside each place to a 'videophone'.

■ **CAKE:** Space Ship

■ **FOOD:** Moon Moguls, Martian Biscuits, Gallactic Discs, Space Spuds, Rock Cakes, UFOs, Meteor Ice-cream Cones

■ **DRINK:** Foaming Crater

■ **GAMES:** Balloon Fight, The Ring Game, Musical Planets (aka Musical Islands), I Went to Mars, Spaceship Eating Race (aka Doughnut Eating Race)

■ **PRIZES:** Sheets of glow-in-the-dark star stickers, Star Trek collector cards.

Please come to my party. Date RSVP Time Address

Here are twenty themes to choose from, enough to cater for most ages and interests

DINOSAURS

■ **DECORATIONS:** Spread brown sheeting 'mud' on the floor, or hessian, anchored down by stones to create a 'primeval swamp'. Hang green and brown streamers from the ceiling and walls, some straight and some curled. Brighten things up with some splashy 'primeval flowers' cut from coloured cardboard.
■ **CAKE:** Dino the Dinosaur
■ **FOOD:** Rocky Road, Cavemen Clubs, Swamp Mud, Baby Burgers, Dinosaur Eggs, Meatballs
■ **DRINK:** Foaming Crater
■ **GAMES:** Pin the Tail on the Triceratops, Colour the Dinosaur, On the Bank, In the Swamp (aka On the Bank, In the River), Hot Volcanic Rock (aka Hot Potato), Hot Rock Relay (aka Hot Potato Relay), Making Words
■ **PRIZES:** Plastic dinosaurs, dinosaur stickers, dinosaur activity books.

PIRATES

■ **DECORATIONS:** Inside, a pirate ship, with big round portholes around the walls, showing waves and sky. The table should be bare, with food laid out on wooden chopping boards and plain platters. Outside, make a Treasure Island by using stuffed toys such as a monkey or a brightly coloured parrot in a tree.
■ **CAKE:** Treasure Chest
■ **FOOD:** Meatballs, Sausage Rolls, Corny Cheese Row Boats, Pirate Face Biscuits
■ **DRINK:** Poison Potion
■ **GAMES:** Treasure Hunt, Thieves Back-to-Back Race, When-the-Music-Stops games played to sea shanties, Musical Islands, Long John Silver Says (aka Simon Says), The Captain's Coming
■ **PRIZES:** Bags of treasure containing plastic coins, eye patches, pirate hats, cardboard swords, books about pirates such as *Kidnapped* or *Peter Pan*.

BEACH

■ **DECORATIONS:** Arrange beach umbrellas, banana chairs, directors' chairs and beach towels around the party area. Hang up crepe paper palm trees and green, yellow and blue balloons; scatter around stuffed animals such as monkeys, snakes and colourful parrots. Alternatively, arrange to take the party to the beach; make sure you set up in a shaded area, take plenty of sunscreen and supervise all swimming and water play.

■ **CAKE:** Sunshine Cake

■ **FOOD:** Prawn Toasts, Frozen Banana Bites, Sunburst Parfait, Hot Dog Boats, Beach Baby Jellies, Ham and Pineapple Pinwheels

■ **DRINK:** Pineapple Cream Crush

■ **GAMES:** Hot Potato, Postman's Island Holiday, On the Sand, in the Sea (aka On the Bank, In the River), Limbo Dancing, Tug of War, Slow Tortoise Race, Oranges and Lemons

■ **PRIZES:** Grass skirts, sun hats, pots of sun cream and coloured zinc, novelty sunglasses.

Cut along the dotted line and come to Sophie's beach party at Balmoral Beach December 6th at 3pm. R.S.V.P......

SNOW

■ **DECORATIONS:** Cover furniture with white sheets; decorate walls with white streamers and balloons; hang paper doilies (representing snowflakes) from the ceiling; tear up white paper to make snow or use white confetti; to simulate a fire tape scrunched-up red cellophane in a corner or a disused fireplace.

■ **CAKE:** Pete the Penguin

■ **FOOD:** Frosted Brownies, Meatballs, Coconut Ice, Pizza, Snowmen

■ **DRINK:** Chocolate Float

■ **GAMES:** Hat Making, Musical Hats, Apple Paring, Frozen Bunnies (aka Wobbling Bunnies), Scavenger Hunt, The Chocolate Game

SPECIAL ACTIVITY: if you live in a snow-prone area and it happens to snow at the time of the party, make playing in the snow the main feature of the party. Have snowman-making contests, toboggan races and snow fights.

■ **PRIZES:** Snow storms (various scenes), woollen gloves, mittens or socks.

Please come to my party.
Date..............
Time..............
Address...........
......
RSVP..............

ZOO

DECORATIONS: Tack large pieces of butchers' paper to walls and invite children to draw an animal mural; place PLEASE DO NOT FEED THE ANIMALS sign over food table, place large stuffed animals—bears, giraffes, lions, and so on—around the party area; use animal or jungle-style glasses and tableware.

■ **CAKES:** Loopy Lion

■ **FOOD:** Animal Crisps, Chicken Nuggets, Zebra Sandwiches, Camel Humps, Chocolate Haystacks, Fruit Jelly Shapes

■ **DRINK:** Jungle Juice

■ **GAMES:** Animal Follow the Leader (confine game to animal movements), Froggy, Froggy May We Cross Your Shining River?, Making Words, Musical Hotch Potch, No Paws Allowed, Animalia

SPECIAL ACTIVITY: video screening of film or cartoon featuring animals.

■ **PRIZES:** Animal puzzles, small plastic or stuffed animals, books about animals, sheets of animal stickers.

ROBOTS & COMPUTERS

■ **DECORATIONS:** Tape a row of cut-out cardboard tools and instruments leading to party area; use aluminium foil to decorate walls and table; tape button-style sweets to table settings to represent control panels.

■ **CAKE:** Robbie the Robot

■ **FOOD:** Kids' Style Nachos, Buttered Corn Cobs, Potato Wedges, Gallactic Discs, Choc-chip Crackles, Toffee Muesli Bars

■ **DRINK:** Motor Oil

■ **GAMES:** Follow the Leader, Three-legged Race, Missing Components (aka Scavenger Race), Blindfold Drawing, Musical Sets, Mystery Parcel

■ **PRIZES:** plastic toy mobile phones, toy robots, toy tools, hand-held computer games.

Halloween

■ **Decorations:** Cover walls and table with black cloth, then drape lightly with glittery net; dim lights and cover windows with orange or green cellophane; suspend black balloons, plastic spiders and bats from the ceiling; place large jack-o'-lanterns and black candles on the table; use black tableware and napkins

■ **Cake:** Jack-o'-Lantern

■ **Food:** Bat Wings, Scary Face Pikelets, Mouse Traps, Frozen Goo, Bleeding Fingers, Squelch and Crunch, Blood Baths

■ **Drink:** Witches' Brew

■ **Games:** Blindman's Buff, The Boiler Burst!, Musical Blackout, Guess in the Dark, Broomstick Relay, Jump the Broom, Musical Torch

SPECIAL ACTIVITY: tell ghost stories

■ **Prizes:** Plastic vampire teeth, magic-shop tricks, packs of cards.

Please come to a HALLOWEEN party at 6pm - 12pm ....

on October 31 at 4 Bat Lane.

RSVP ....

Arabian Nights

■ **Decorations:** Move all the furniture out of the room and place a 'magic' carpet in the middle of the floor; cover carpet with cushions; drape walls with colourful cloth for a tent effect; serve food on a low table.

■ **Cake:** Magic Carpet

■ **Food:** Banana, Nut and Date Fingers, Camel Humps, Starry Night Crisps, Mini Pizzas

■ **Drink:** Cool Breeze

■ **Games:** Musical Magic Carpet, Musical Cushions (aka Musical Chairs), Magic Lantern, Gods and Goddesses, Pin the Tail on the Camel, I Asked the Genie of the Lamp (aka I Went to Mars)

SPECIAL ACTIVITY: storytelling from *1001 Nights*

■ **Prizes:** Plastic jewellery, exotic scarves and headdresses, bubble pipes.

Please come to my party.
Time ....
Date ....
Address .... RSVP

PLEASE COME
TO MY PARTY!
theme . . . .
date . . . . . . time . . . . . .
address . . . .
. . . .
RSVP . . . .

Hippies

Come to Jills on 7th January at ♥ for a birthday party! Groovy! R.S.V.P

THE GreaT OUTDOOrs

■ **DECORATIONS:** Choose a characteristic outdoor setting away from the home or set up the barbecue in the backyard.
■ **CAKE:** Snake Cake
■ **FOOD:** Bugs in Rugs, Insy Winsy Spiders, Sausage Sizzle, Onion Dip, Cheese Swags, Maggot Mounds
■ **DRINK:** Ant Cordial
■ **GAMES:** Musical Bumps, Musical Islands, Hot Potato, Scavenger Hunt, Fishing Competition, Pass the Backpack (aka Pass the Parcel)
SPECIAL ACTIVITY: bush walking
■ **PRIZES:** Jumbo jelly snakes, packets of seeds and plastic watering can, ant farm, bug-catcher, butterfly net.

Hippies

■ **DECORATIONS:** Decorate room with Sixties motifs such as posters of Woodstock doves, Jimi Hendrix or Che Guevara; shaggy rugs, macrame light fittings, sea-grass matting, colourful scarves, brass bells on ribbons, tie-dyed and batik fabrics.
■ **CAKE:** Flower Power
■ **FOOD:** Pizza, Crunchy Top Brownies, Vege Sticks and Onion Dip, Psychedelic Fairy Bread, Mud Bath (aka Swamp Mud), Ham and Egg Roll
■ **DRINK:** Banana Smoothie
■ **GAMES:** Hat and Scarf (use hippy clothes), Trivia Contest, Straws and Beans, Nose in Matchbox
SPECIAL ACTIVITY: hair-braiding; face painting (with flowers and peace signs)
■ **PRIZES:** Sew-on jeans patches, peace badges, candles, incense sticks.

TeDDY Bears PicNic

■ **DECORATIONS:** Choose an outdoor area and scatter numerous teddies around it; use a rug for picnic food or a paper tablecloth covered with hand-drawn paw prints; tie balloons to trees.
■ **CAKE:** Tom Teddy
■ **FOOD:** Choc-mint cones, Teddy Bear Cakes, Sticky Banana Buns, Sausage Rolls
■ **DRINK:** Moo Juice.
■ **GAMES:** Teddyback Race, Musical Hotch Potch (with teddy bears), Teddies Bat the Balloon, Pass the Parcel, Farmer in the Dell
■ **PRIZES:** Clutching teddy bears, teddy bear stickers, books on teddy bears, pencils, erasers and notepads featuring teddies.

Dear Georgia,
please come to Harriet's birthday picnic on May 4, down in the woods at Honeypot Park from 2pm to 5pm.
Bring your favourite teddy. You're sure of a big surprise!

CHrisTmas

■ **DECORATIONS:** Decorate eaves, doorways and windows with mistletoe and holly, real or otherwise; decorate Christmas tree; hang red ribbons across window frames.
■ **CAKE:** Christmas Cracker
■ **FOOD:** White Christmas, Prawn Toasts, Stained Glass Biscuits, Sausage Rolls, Frankfurt Bonbons
■ **DRINK:** Rudolph's Punch
■ **GAMES:** Charades, Present Hunt, Trim the Tree, Apple Bobbing, Pass the Parcel, Santa Says (aka Simon Says), Reindeer Race (aka Wheelbarrow Race)
SPECIAL ACTIVITY: Christmas carol singing
■ **PRIZES:** Small presents taken from tree, Christmas tree decorations.

Please come to my party.
Date ....
Time ....
Address ....

RSVP ....

WILD WEST

■ **DECORATIONS:** Set out real bales of hay for seating if party is outdoors. If party is indoors decorate walls or party area with saddles, lariats, cowboy boots, bandanas, Indian rugs and wall hangings, beadwork, pottery or feather headdresses; make forts or wagons from large cardboard boxes; cardboard cut-out cacti on walls; children's play tent can be set up inside as an Indian tepee.
■ **CAKE:** Texas Boot
■ **FOOD:** Guacamole and Corn Chips, Kids' Style Nachos, Buttered Corn Cobs, Potato Wedges, Hot Bean Dogs, Choc-cherry Spiders
■ **DRINK:** Cactus Juice
■ **GAMES:** Tag, Captives, Pin the Tail on the Ornery Mule, Hot Potato, Wobbling Prairie Dogs (aka Wobbling Bunnies)
SPECIAL ACTIVITY: square dancing, 'war-paint' face painting
■ **PRIZES:** Plastic cowboy and Indian sets, sheriff's stars, twirling ropes.

PUNK

■ **DECORATIONS:** Drape black fabric, held with safety pins, on furniture and windows; pin up posters of punk groups such as the Sex Pistols and The Ramones.
■ **CAKE:** Punk Head
■ **FOOD:** Punk Faces, Bleeding Fingers, Choc-cherry Spiders, Sausage Rolls, Mini Pizzas, Ham and Cheese Scrolls
■ **DRINK:** Cola Spider
■ **GAMES:** Musical games (played to punk music), Tug of War, Balloon Flight, Pin the Tail on the Rat, Sid Vicious Sez (aka Simon Says)
■ **PRIZES:** Temporary tattoos, face paint, coloured hair spray, chunky plastic rings and earrings.

SPOrt

■ **DECORATIONS:** Hang up posters of sporting heroes interspersed with sporting caps, pennants, trophies, certificates, and so on; cover table with sports section from newspaper.

■ **CAKE:** Running Shoe

■ **FOOD:** Choc-coated Iceblocks, Toffee Muesli Bars, Meatballs, Ham and Egg Roll, Buttered Corn Cobs

■ **DRINK:** Sports Stamina

■ **GAMES:** High Steppers, Bean Bag Hockey, Overpass, Underpass, Tissue and Straw Race, (Sports) Trivia Quiz, Egg and Spoon Race, Tug of War, Bat the Balloon, Pass the Orange

■ **PRIZES:** Tennis balls, toy golf sets, golf-ball soap, basketball cards.

Alex is invited to Will's sport party at the Sports Centre, on May 23, from 10.30 – 2.30.

RSVP . . . .

CiRCUS

■ **DECORATIONS:** Draw clown faces on bunches of multi-coloured balloons and hang from the ceiling; drape streamers of all colours from a central point, such as a light-fitting, to suggest a circus tent; scatter curled ribbon, coloured confetti, whistles and balloons across party table.

■ **CAKE:** Kooky Klown

■ **FOOD:** Clown Faces, Cherry Crunch, Caramel Popcorn Balls, Frankfurt Bonbons

■ **DRINK:** Mango Wizz

■ **GAMES:** Hop and Pop, Bat the Balloon, Whizzing Balloons, Balloon Hop, Chocolate Game, Laughing Handkerchief, Sack Race, Blindfold Drawing, Squeak, Piggy, Squeak, Follow the Leader

SPECIAL ACTIVITY: visit by a professional clown or magician or the children can put on their own circus, with each performing an act.

■ **PRIZES:** Clown masks or fright wigs, books about the circus, simple magic tricks, clown fridge magnets.

Please come to my party.
Date . . . . Time . . . .
Address . . . .
Phone . . . . RSVP
Please dress as a circus performer.
Faces will be painted at door.

DISCO

■ **DECORATIONS:** Replace standard light globes with coloured light globes, hang up party lights, put up posters of disco groups and singers.

■ **CAKE:** The Amp

■ **FOOD:** Choc-chip Fudge, Pizza, American Hot Dogs

■ **DRINK:** Malted Milkshake

■ **GAMES:** Musical games to disco music, Mystery Parcel, Magpies, Chocolate Game, Doughnut Eating Race, (Music) Trivia Quiz

SPECIAL ACTIVITY: badge making using pictures from fanzines and a badge maker (borrowed from a local club or school, or hired for the party).

■ **PRIZES:** Fake fingernails, glitter, face paint, cheap glitzy earrings, sunglasses.

UNDERWATER

■ **DECORATIONS:** Decorate walls or pool area with multi-coloured cardboard fish and sea creatures; float appropriate bath toys in pool; hang blue or green streamers from clothesline; use plates, cups and napkins with fish motifs.

■ **CAKE:** Funny Fish

■ **FOOD:** Cheese and Salmon Tarts, Fish Cocktails, Life Savers, Sunken Subs, Fishermen's Burgers, Speckled Bubble Bars, Hot Dog Boats

■ **DRINK:** Fruit Punch

■ **GAMES:** Apple Bobbing, Water Race, Fishing Competition, Flying Fish, Crocodile Race, On the Bank, in the River, Sardines, What's the Time, Mister Sea Monster? (aka What's the Time, Mister Wolf?)

SPECIAL ACTIVITY: blowing bubbles, water fight or pool play

■ **PRIZES:** Swimming goggles, pots of zinc cream, floating bath toys, fish-shaped bath sponges.

CaKe recipes

BASIC **BUTTERCAKE**

Preparation time: 20 minutes *Total cooking time:*
35–40 minutes *Makes* one 23 cm square or round cake
(or 28 x 18 cm rectangular cake)

150 g butter ▲ **^{3}/4 cup caster sugar** ▲ **3 eggs** ▲ **1 teaspoon
imitation vanilla essence** ▲ **1^2/3 cups self-raising flour**
▲ **^{1}/3 cup milk**

1 Preheat oven to moderate 180°C. Brush tin with melted
butter or oil. Line base and side with baking paper.
2 Using electric beaters, beat butter and sugar in small
mixing bowl until light and creamy. Add eggs gradually,
beating thoroughly after each addition. Add essence; beat
until combined.
3 Using a metal spoon, fold in sifted flour alternately with
milk. Stir until just combined and mixture is smooth. (Be
careful not to overmix.)
4 Spoon mixture into prepared tin; smooth surface. Bake
35–40 minutes or until a skewer comes out clean when it is
inserted in centre of cake. Leave cake in tin 5 minutes before
turning onto wire rack to cool.
NOTE: The above quantity can be adapted to most sizes of
cake tin. Make up 1^1/2 quantities of mixture for a 20 x 30 cm
tin, and 2 quantities for a Swiss roll tin. When using a Swiss
roll tin, line the tin with baking paper extending 3 cm over
each edge. Use any leftover cake mixture for patty cakes.

FLUFFY ICING

Preparation time: 15 minutes *Total cooking time:* 5 minutes
Makes one quantity

1^1/4 cups caster sugar ■ **^{1}/2 cup water** ■ **3 egg whites**

1 Combine sugar and water in small pan. Stir constantly over
low heat until mixture boils and sugar has dissolved. Simmer,
uncovered, without stirring 5 minutes.
2 Using electric beaters, beat egg whites in a clean, dry
mixing bowl until stiff peaks form.
3 Pour hot syrup in a thin stream over egg whites, beating
constantly until icing is thick, glossy and increased in volume.

BASIC **BUTTERCREAM**

Preparation time: 15 minutes *Total cooking time:* Nil
Makes one quantity

250 g butter ◆ **1^1/3 cups icing sugar, sifted** ◆ **2 tablespoons
warm milk**

1 Beat butter in small mixing bowl until light and creamy.
2 Gradually add sugar and milk,
beating for 5 minutes or until
mixture is smooth,
light and creamy.

Jack-o'-Lantern, page 28

*Dino the Dinosaur,
page 22*

Kooky Klown, page 36

With a basic cake and some icing, you have the makings of spectacular party cakes

CARROT CAKE

Preparation time: 30 minutes *Total cooking time:* 1 hour
Makes one 20 cm square cake

2 cups grated carrot • 1/2 cup sultanas • 2/3 cup chopped
walnuts • 1 cup caster sugar • 3 eggs, lightly beaten • 3/4 cup
vegetable oil • 2 cups self-raising flour • 2 teaspoons mixed
spice • 2 teaspoons ground ginger • 1 teaspoon ground
cinnamon • 1 teaspoon bicarbonate of soda

1 Preheat oven to moderate 180°C. Brush deep 20 cm square
cake tin with melted butter or oil; line base with baking
paper. Place carrot, sultanas, walnuts and sugar in large bowl.
Add combined eggs and oil.
2 Add sifted flour, spices and soda. Combine with wooden
spoon.
3 Pour into prepared tin, smooth surface. Bake for 1 hour or
until skewer comes out clean when inserted into centre.
Leave in tin for 10 minutes before turning onto wire rack
to cool.
NOTE:: Use Carrot Cake as an alternative to Basic
Buttercake, if desired. Decorate and store as for Buttercake.

NOTE: Fluffy Icing and Basic Buttercream should be coloured
and used immediately (before it begins to harden and set.)
Once iced and decorated the cake can be stored for several
hours in a cool, dark place. Do not refrigerate cakes covered
with Fluffy Icing as this will make the surface sticky, and
icing may begin to separate.

WARNING
Use bamboo skewers to construct cakes, and
always remove them before serving. NEVER use
toothpicks to hold cakes together. They can easily
get lost in a serving and a child can choke on them
or be injured and distressed by them.

Sunshine Cake, page 24

Spaceship, page 21

Loopy Lion, page 26

party cakes

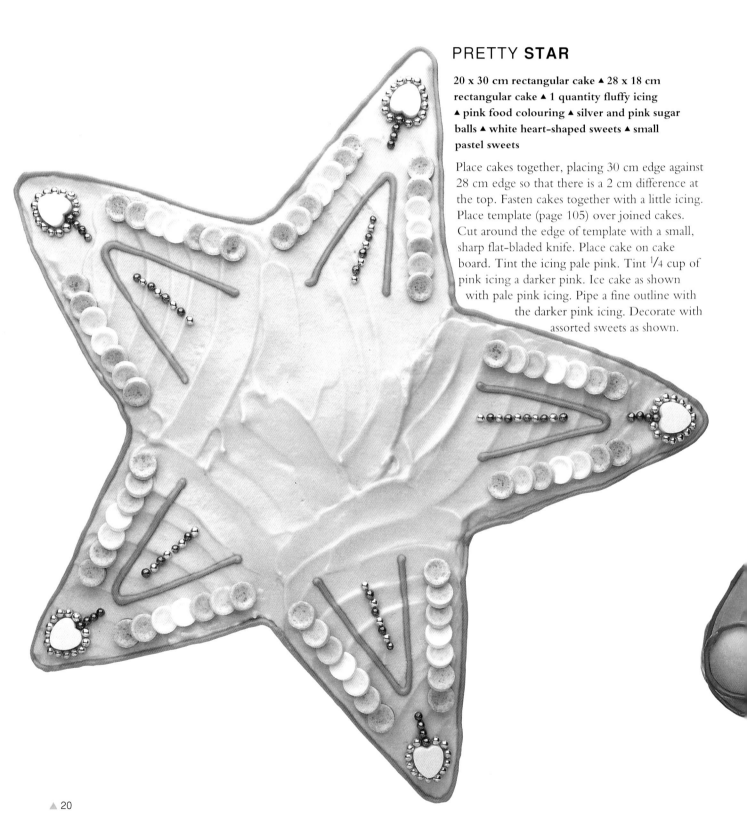

PRETTY **STAR**

20 x 30 cm rectangular cake ▲ 28 x 18 cm rectangular cake ▲ 1 quantity fluffy icing ▲ pink food colouring ▲ silver and pink sugar balls ▲ white heart-shaped sweets ▲ small pastel sweets

Place cakes together, placing 30 cm edge against 28 cm edge so that there is a 2 cm difference at the top. Fasten cakes together with a little icing. Place template (page 105) over joined cakes. Cut around the edge of template with a small, sharp flat-bladed knife. Place cake on cake board. Tint the icing pale pink. Tint $1/4$ cup of pink icing a darker pink. Ice cake as shown with pale pink icing. Pipe a fine outline with the darker pink icing. Decorate with assorted sweets as shown.

Making a fun shape from a simple buttercake and a few sweets is easier than it looks

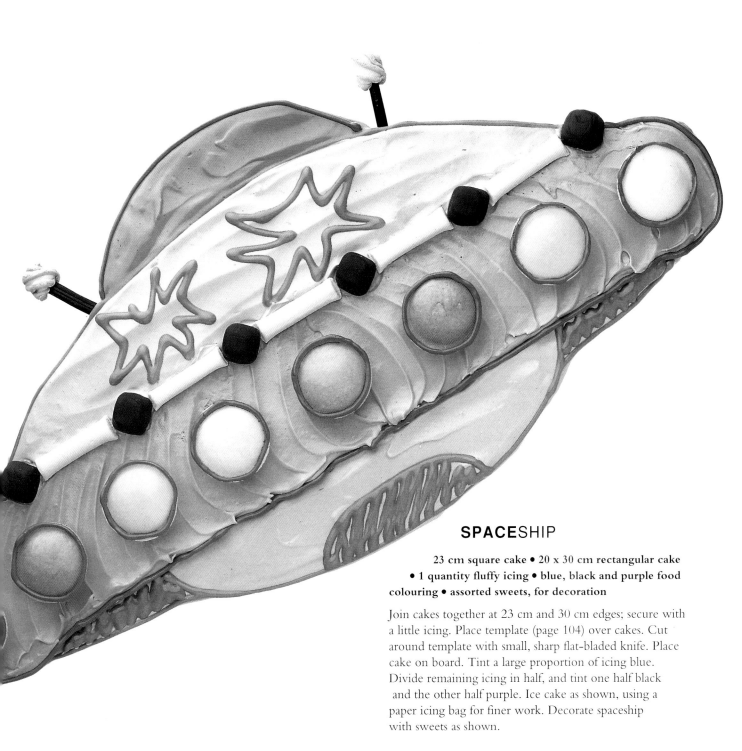

SPACESHIP

23 cm square cake • 20 x 30 cm rectangular cake • 1 quantity fluffy icing • blue, black and purple food colouring • assorted sweets, for decoration

Join cakes together at 23 cm and 30 cm edges; secure with a little icing. Place template (page 104) over cakes. Cut around template with small, sharp flat-bladed knife. Place cake on board. Tint a large proportion of icing blue. Divide remaining icing in half, and tint one half black and the other half purple. Ice cake as shown, using a paper icing bag for finer work. Decorate spaceship with sweets as shown.

DINO THE DINOSAUR

23 cm square cake ◆ 20 x 30 cm rectangular cake ◆ 2 quantities basic buttercream ◆ blue and black food colouring ◆ purple Smarties, for body ◆ white jellybeans, for eyes

Join cakes together at short sides; secure with a little icing. Place template (page 106) over cakes. Cut around template with small, sharp flat-bladed knife. Tint buttercream blue, leaving a small portion plain and tinting the other portion black. Place cake on board. Ice cake as shown. Decorate with sweets. Outline with fine lines of black icing.

TREASURE **CHEST**

**2 x (20 x 30 cm) rectangular cakes ● 1¹/₂ quantities
basic buttercream ● pink and black food colouring
● licorice strap, for trunk ● assorted sweets, for treasure
● string of pearls, for decoration**

Join cakes together at long sides; secure with a little icing.
Place template (page 106) over cakes. Cut around template
with a small, sharp flat-bladed knife. Place cake on board. With
a fine skewer, poke holes through template to give dotted
outline for icing. Tint a large portion of icing pink; divide the
the remainder in two. Tint one portion pale pink and the
remainder black. Ice cake as shown. Pipe with a black outline.
Cut licorice strap for trunk. Pipe fine lines of icing for
stitching. Decorate trunk with assorted sweets and pearls.

SUNSHINE CAKE

2 x (20 x 30 cm) rectangular cakes ▲ 2 quantities basic buttercream ▲ yellow and orange food colouring ▲ assorted sweets, for face

Place cakes together at long sides; secure with a little icing. Place template (page 107) over cakes. Cut around template with small, sharp flat–bladed knife. Place cake on board. Tint icing bright yellow. Tint a small portion of yellow icing orange. Ice cake with yellow as shown. Wipe strokes of orange icing randomly around cake to give highlights. Decorate cake with sweets as shown.

PETE THE PENGUIN

**23 cm square cake ■ 20 x 30 cm rectangular cake
■ 1½ quantities buttercream ■ black, yellow and blue
food colouring ■ white chocolate disc, for eye ■ small
marshmallow, for inner eye ■ small black jellybean,
halved, for pupil ■ orange snake, for mouth**

Place cakes together at short sides; secure with a
little icing. Place template (page 107) over cakes.
Cut around template with a small, sharp flat-
bladed knife. Place cake on board. Poke holes
through template with a fine skewer to
trace cake design onto cake surface.
Tint icing to required colours
and ice cake as shown.
Decorate with sweets
as shown.

LOOPY **LION**

2 x (20 x 30 cm) rectangular cakes
- 1½ **quantities buttercream**
- 100 g **dark chocolate, melted**
- **caramel brown food colouring**
- 2 **large white marshmallows, for eyes**
- 2 **caramel buds, for ears**
- 1 **large milk chocolate disc, for nose**
- 2 **brown smarties, for eyes**
- **licorice strap for tail, mouth and whiskers**
- **red sweet for mouth**

Put cakes together at long sides; secure with a little icing. Place template (page 102) over cakes. Cut around edge of template with a small, sharp flat-bladed knife. Poke holes through template with a fine skewer to mark outline of face. The dotted line will act as a guide when icing. Divide buttercream in half. Beat melted chocolate into one half of buttercream. Divide the remaining plain buttercream into 2 portions. Tint one portion caramel brown and the other a pale beige. Ice cake as shown. Decorate with assorted sweets.

ROBBIE THE ROBOT

2 x (20 x 30 cm) rectangular cakes
• 2 quantities fluffy icing • purple and peach
food colouring • licorice strap, cut finely
• assorted sweets for face and body

Put cakes together at long sides; secure
with a little icing. Place template
(page 102) over cakes. Cut
around template using a small,
sharp flat-bladed knife. Place
cake on board. Poke holes
through template with a fine
skewer to mark outline of face.
Tint $\frac{3}{4}$ of the icing purple and the
remainder pale peach. Ice cake and
decorate with sweets as shown.

JACK-**O**'-LANTERN

**2 x 23 cm square cakes ▲ 1 quantity basic buttercream
▲ orange and black food colouring ▲ black licorice strap,
for facial features**

Put cakes together; secure with a little icing. Place template
(page 100) over cakes. Cut around template with a sharp,
flat-bladed knife. Place cake on board. Tint a small portion of
buttercream pale orange. Tint $1/4$ of remaining buttercream
black and the rest bright orange. Ice cake as shown. Pipe fine
lines with black icing. Cut licorice strap with sharp scissors or
knife. (Licorice strap can also be cut into fine strips for
outline in place of piping.)
NOTE: You can use two Swiss roll tin sized cakes if
you prefer. Spread one cake with a little jam and lay
the other on top. Lay template on
cakes and follow
procedure as above.

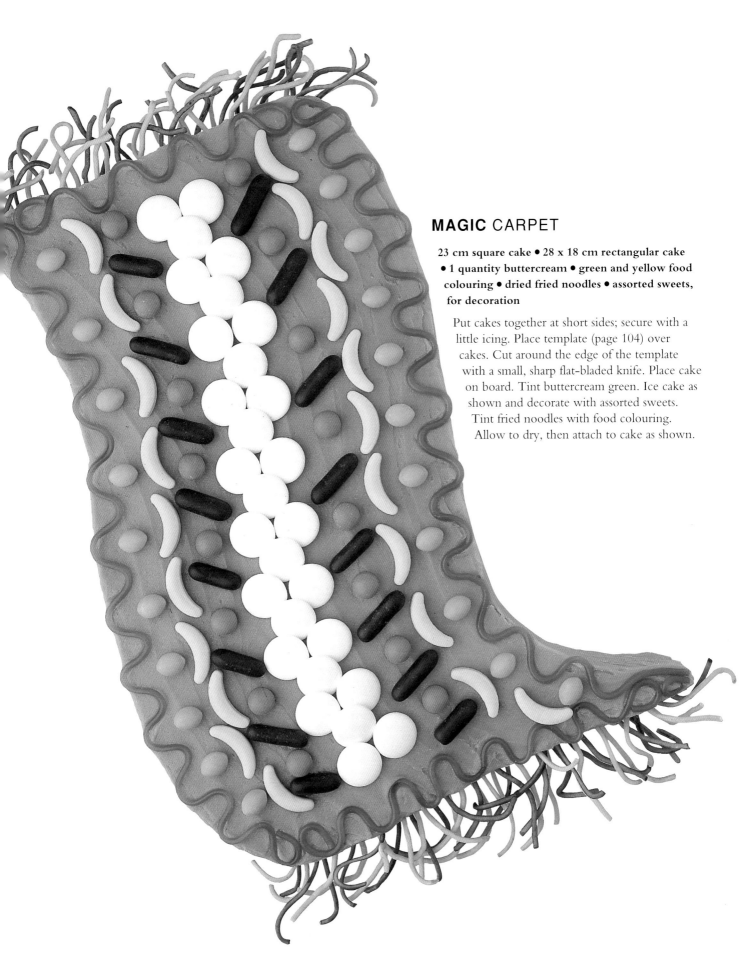

MAGIC CARPET

**23 cm square cake • 28 x 18 cm rectangular cake
• 1 quantity buttercream • green and yellow food
colouring • dried fried noodles • assorted sweets,
for decoration**

Put cakes together at short sides; secure with a
little icing. Place template (page 104) over
cakes. Cut around the edge of the template
with a small, sharp flat-bladed knife. Place cake
on board. Tint buttercream green. Ice cake as
shown and decorate with assorted sweets.
Tint fried noodles with food colouring.
Allow to dry, then attach to cake as shown.

SNAKE CAKE

250 g dark chocolate melts, melted ▲ 250 g milk chocolate melts, melted ▲ 250 g white chocolate melts, melted ▲ 2 x (20 x 30 cm) rectangular cakes ▲ 2 quantities buttercream ▲ 250 g dark chocolate, melted ▲ caramel–brown food colouring ▲ large white chocolate buttons, or discs ▲ licorice strap cut into thin strips, for outline and eyelashes ▲ small black jellybean, halved, for eyes ▲ orange jube, cut, for mouth

Line several oven trays with baking paper. Pipe small, medium and large dark chocolate buttons onto trays. Allow to set. Peel off paper and repeat with milk and white chocolate. Use small paper icing bags to do this and discard bags after use. (Make several bags before melting chocolate. Change bags when necessary.)

Join cakes together at long sides; secure with a little icing. Place template (page 103) over cake. Cut around template with small, sharp flat-bladed knife. Place cake on board. Beat melted chocolate into ²/₃ of the buttercream. Ice head and body of snake. Reserve 2 tablespoons of any remaining icing; tint caramel-brown. Ice cake as shown. Decorate with chocolate buttons and sweets for face, as shown.

HINT: As an alternative to making them, buy small, medium and large chocolate buttons in white, milk and dark.

FLOWER **POWER**

20 x 30 cm rectangular cake ◆ 28 x 18 cm rectangular cake (or 20 cm square cake) ◆ 1 quantity fluffy icing ◆ yellow and pink food colouring ◆ coloured sugar balls

Join cakes together at short sides; secure with a little icing. Place template (page 100) over cakes. Cut around template with a small, sharp flat-bladed knife. Place cake on board. Tint a small portion of icing pink and the remainder yellow. Tint a small portion of yellow icing darker for outline. Ice cake as shown. Decorate centre with sugar balls.

TOM TEDDY

20 x 30 cm rectangular cake ■ 23 cm square cake ■ 1^1/$_2$ quantities buttercream ■ 250 g dark chocolate, melted ■ ^{1}/$_2$ quantity fluffy icing ■ brown food colouring ■ assorted sweets for face

Join cakes together at 20 and 23 cm edges; secure with a little icing. Place template (page 103) over cakes. Cut around templates with small, sharp flat-bladed knife. Place cake on board. With a skewer, poke holes in top of cake through template to trace an outline of face. Beat melted chocolate into buttercream with electric beaters. Reserve ^{1}/$_4$ cup chocolate buttercream and tint dark brown with food colouring. Tint fluffy icing caramel brown. Ice cake as shown. Decorate with sweets for face. Use a skewer or fork to fluff edge of darker icing to emphasise the fur.

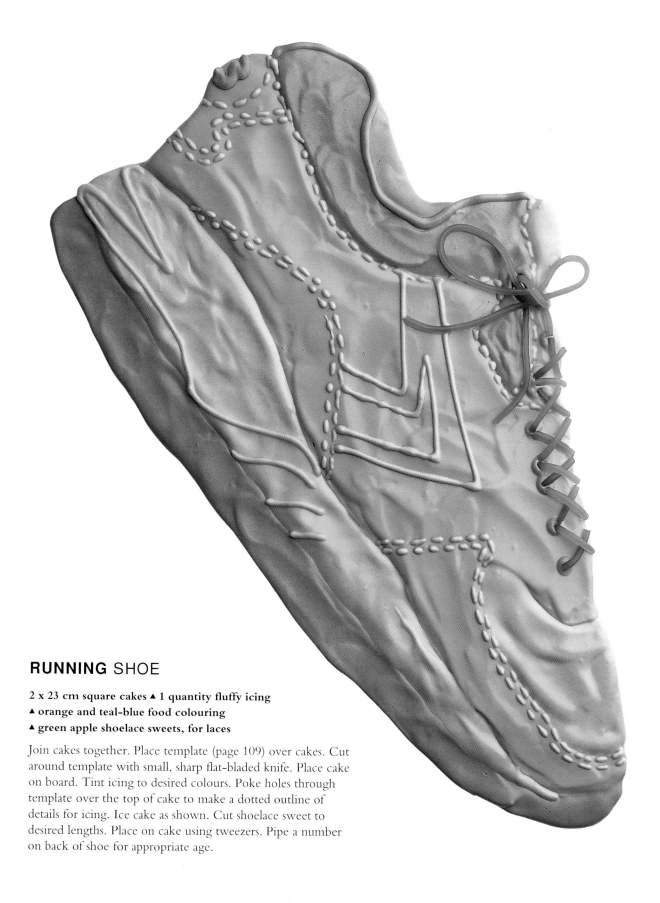

RUNNING SHOE

2 x 23 cm square cakes ▲ 1 quantity fluffy icing
▲ orange and teal-blue food colouring
▲ green apple shoelace sweets, for laces

Join cakes together. Place template (page 109) over cakes. Cut
around template with small, sharp flat-bladed knife. Place cake
on board. Tint icing to desired colours. Poke holes through
template over the top of cake to make a dotted outline of
details for icing. Ice cake as shown. Cut shoelace sweet to
desired lengths. Place on cake using tweezers. Pipe a number
on back of shoe for appropriate age.

TEXAS BOOT

20 x 30 cm rectangular cake ■ **20 cm square cake**
■ **1¹/₂ quantities buttercream** ■ **red food colouring**
■ **licorice strap, twists and all-sorts, for decoration**
■ **small yellow and orange sweets** ■ **toy silver star, for spur**

Join cakes together at short sides; secure with a little icing.
Place template (page 105) over cakes. Cut around template
with small, sharp flat-bladed knife. Place cake on board. Tint
icing bright red. Ice cake as shown. Cut licorice for
decoration. Decorate as shown.

PUNK **HEAD**

**2 x 20 cm square cakes ▲ 2 quantities buttercream
▲ green, orange and peach food colouring
▲ licorice strap ▲ coloured sugar balls
▲ white sweet, for eye ▲ small black jelly bean,
halved ▲ purple snake, for mouth
▲ small and large safety pins**

Place cakes together; secure with a little icing.
Place template (page 108) over cake. Cut
around the edge of template with a small,
sharp flat-bladed knife. Place cake on board.
Tint ¼ of the icing green, another
¼ orange. Tint remaining icing pale peach,
reserving 2 tablespoons to tint a darker peach.
Ice cake as shown. Cut licorice strap into thin
strips for outline of hair and ear. Cut another piece
for an eyebrow. Attach safety pins to licorice strap
for the neck band. Decorate with sweets as shown.

CHRISTMAS CRACKER

**2 x (18 x 28 cm) rectangular cakes ✦ 1 quantity fluffy icing
✦ green food colouring ✦ coloured sugar balls ✦ red and green
ribbon ✦ gold or silver cardboard cut into tree shapes ✦ non-toxic
glitter glue, to decorate cardboard trees ✦ coloured star stickers,
for cardboard trees ✦ small pieces of licorice strap**

Place cakes together at the short sides; secure with a little icing.
Place template (page 108) over cake. Cut around edge of
template with a small, sharp flat-bladed knife. Place cake on
board. Tint icing green. Reserve about ¼ cup and tint this a
darker green. Ice cake as shown. Decorate with cardboard
Christmas trees, silver balls and small licorice pieces. Pipe a fine
outline with dark green icing. Place ribbons on last.

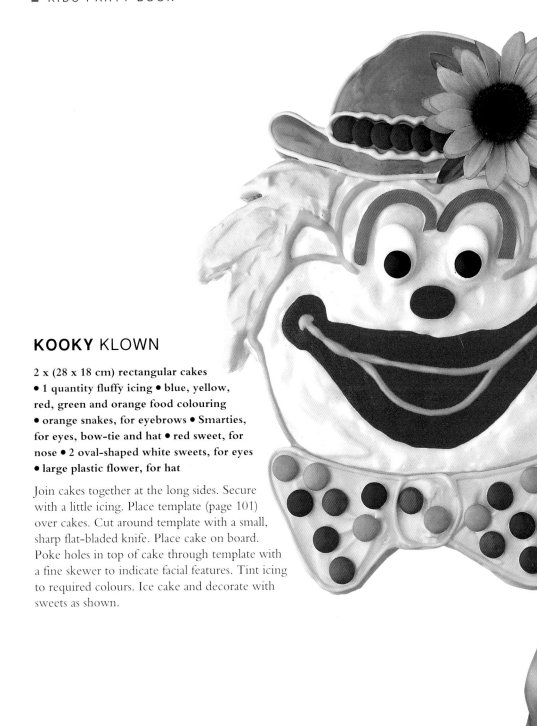

KOOKY KLOWN

**2 x (28 x 18 cm) rectangular cakes
• 1 quantity fluffy icing • blue, yellow,
red, green and orange food colouring
• orange snakes, for eyebrows • Smarties,
for eyes, bow-tie and hat • red sweet, for
nose • 2 oval-shaped white sweets, for eyes
• large plastic flower, for hat**

Join cakes together at the long sides. Secure
with a little icing. Place template (page 101)
over cakes. Cut around template with a small,
sharp flat-bladed knife. Place cake on board.
Poke holes in top of cake through template with
a fine skewer to indicate facial features. Tint icing
to required colours. Ice cake and decorate with
sweets as shown.

FUNNY FISH

**2 x 23 cm square cakes ▲ 1 quantity fluffy icing ▲ green, orange
and yellow food colouring ▲ large chocolate disc, for eye
▲ oval peach-coloured sweet, for eye ▲ blue Smartie, for eye**

Join cakes together. Place template (page 101) over cakes. Cut
around the edge of template with a small, sharp flat-bladed
knife. Place cake on board. Leave small portion of icing white.
Divide remaining icing between three bowls; tint yellow, green
and orange. Ice cake as shown. Decorate with sweets as shown.

THE **AMP**

20 x 30 cm rectangular cake ■ 1 quantity buttercream ■ blue and yellow food colouring ■ 100 g white chocolate melts, melted ■ 50 g dark chocolate melts, melted ■ yellow twisted licorice allsort

Place template (page 109) over cake. Trim cake to size. Place cake on board. Mark circles on cake. Using a small, sharp knife cut out speaker holes to a depth of 2 cm. Remove cake inside circles and discard. Tint ⅔ buttercream blue and remainder yellow. Ice cake as shown. Line a tray with baking paper. Pipe white and dark chocolate musical notes and treble clefs onto paper. Allow chocolate to set. Tint remaining white chocolate blue. Trace speaker holes onto tracing paper. Pipe the outline of the circles with blue chocolate. Pipe a lattice pattern inside outline and allow to set. Carefully lift chocolate shapes off paper and arrange on cake, placing lattice circles over speaker holes. Place a slice of licorice allsort in each corner.

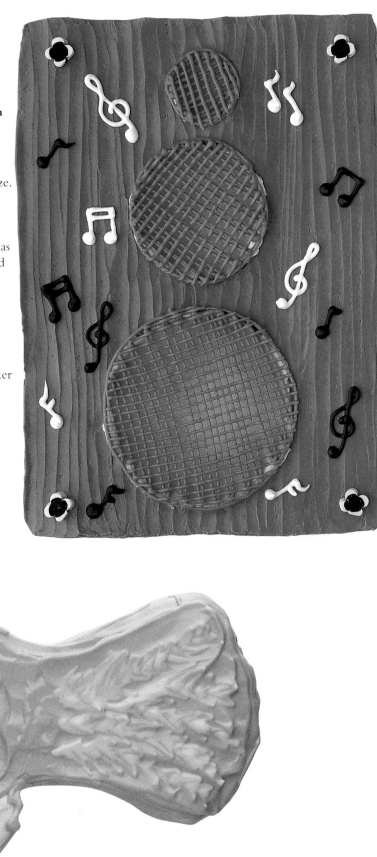

ONE: SOLDIER

2 x (26 x 8 x 4.5 cm) long bar cakes ▲ 1 jam Swiss roll, for Buzby hat ▲ 1 quantity buttercream ▲ red, blue, black food colouring ▲ 1 large white marshmallow, cut in half ▲ 1 twisted marshmallow ▲ apricot roll-ups ▲ small yellow jelly beans, cut in half

Cut cakes into shapes as shown in diagram below. With scissors, cut out roll-ups for shoulders, cuffs, belt and side panels. Ice cake as shown. Ice shoes with a double layer so icing is raised slightly. Pipe black outline to define.

TWO: SNAKE

26 x 8 x 4.5 cm long bar cake ■ 20 cm ring cake ■ 1 quantity buttercream ■ brown food colouring ■ Smarties ■ white marshmallow, halved ■ black licorice strap, for mouth ■ green roll-up, for tongue ■ hundreds and thousands ■ small black jelly bean or bullet, cut in half for eyes.

Cut cakes into shapes as shown in diagram below. Leave ¼ cup icing plain; tint the remainder brown. Ice cake as shown. Pipe swirls of white icing as shown. Fill gaps with hundreds and thousands. Decorate with Smarties and other sweets for face.

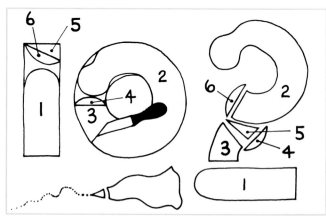

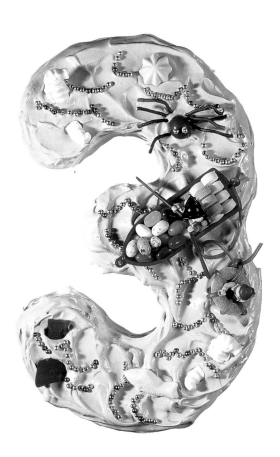

THREE: SEA

2 x 20 cm ring cakes ◆ 1 quantity fluffy icing ◆ blue and brown food colouring ◆ coloured sugar balls ◆ seahorse, fish, starfish and shell-shaped sweets ◆ chocolate malt balls ◆ fried noodles ◆ green jelly ring ◆ green apple shoelace strips ◆ toy boat, filled with small jelly beans and other small sweets ◆ pirate and soldier toys

Cut cakes into shapes as shown in diagram below. Tint icing pale blue. Ice cake as shown. Swirl icing to make the waves. Decorate tops of swirls with silver balls. Cut seahorses in half. Press into icing. Place a small toy in jelly ring to resemble a life buoy. Attach to boat with green shoelace strip. Place boat on cake. Tint fried noodles with brown food colouring. Use for octopus tentacles.

FOUR: DOLL

3 x (26 x 8 x 4.5 cm) bar cakes ● 1 quantity buttercream ● red, pink and brown food colouring ● fried noodles for hair ● pink Smarties, for cheeks ● small white marshmallows (cut in half), for eyes ● blue and brown 'gourmet' jelly beans (halved), for nose and eyes ● hundreds and thousands, for vest ● flat raspberry straps (cut in thin strips), for bows ● green apple shoelace strips ● red snake, for mouth ● green sweets, for buttons ● yellow sweet iced with a '4', for vest

Cut cakes into shapes as shown in diagram below. Tint a small portion of buttercream red and another brown. Leave about $1/2$ cup plain and tint the remainder pale pink. Ice cake as shown. Pipe a fine brown outline for the vest and shirt. Pipe fine red stripes for skirt. Press fried noodles into cake for hair. Decorate with sweets as shown.

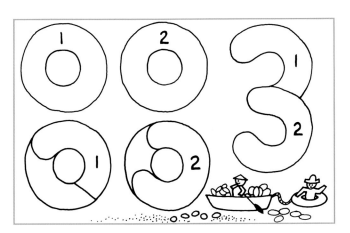

FIVE: TRAIN

20 cm ring cake ▲ 26 x 8 x 4.5 cm bar cake ▲ 1 jam rollette ▲ 1 quantity buttercream ▲ red and yellow food colouring ▲ licorice allsorts ▲ candy bananas ▲ coloured popcorn ▲ jubes ▲ barley sugar ▲ licorice bullets ▲ Smarties ▲ green snake ▲ marshmallows ▲ large chocolate buttons or melts, for wheels ▲ licorice strap, for cabin ▲ white Lifesaver, for cabin ▲ licorice pieces ▲ cotton wool, for steam

Cut cakes into shapes as shown in diagram below. Reserve 1/2 cup buttercream; colour remainder with melted chocolate. Beat until smooth. Tint half reserved icing red, and other half yellow. Cut cake and ice as shown. Trim rollette to sit flat on cabin; cover with chocolate buttercream. Join with licorice pieces. Decorate with sweets, as shown.

SIX: SKATEBOARDER

20 cm ring cake ■ 26 x 8 x 4.5 cm bar cake ■ 1 quantity buttercream ■ blue, yellow and caramel-brown food colouring ■ green and yellow roll-ups ■ Smarties ■ oval chocolates, for shoes ■ small black jelly beans, for wheels and eyes ■ orange snakes, for arms and legs ■ marshmallows, for socks and shirt collar ■ licorice strap, for hair ■ red snake, for mouth ■ pink candy, for shorts ■ hundreds and thousands

Cut cakes into shapes as shown in diagram below. Reserve 1/3 cup buttercream and tint the remainder blue. Tint a third of the reserved buttercream brown and the remainder yellow. Ice cake as shown. With scissors, cut snakes for hands and legs. Cut roll-ups for hat and skateboard. Decorate with sweets as shown.

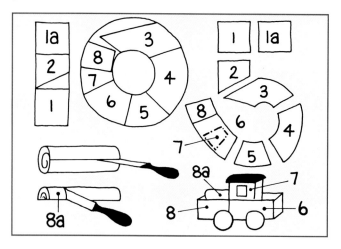

SEVEN: PALM TREE

**2 x (26 x 8 x 4.5 cm) long bar cakes ◆ 1 quantity buttercream
◆ small and large candy bananas ◆ green mint leaves
◆ dark green roll-ups ◆ blue, green and yellow food colouring
◆ toy bird**

Cut cakes into shapes as shown in diagram below. Reserve
1/4 cup buttercream and tint blue. Divide the remaining
buttercream in half. Tint one portion yellow and the other
green. Ice cake as shown. Cut mint leaves in half lengthways.
Cut roll-ups into large palm-leaf shapes. Decorate tree with
leaves and bananas. Place toy bird in tree. Tint a small
portion of leftover yellow icing darker. Spread randomly over
tree trunk for bark effect.

NUMBER EIGHT: FAIRY

**20 cm round cake ● 20 cm ring cake ● 1 quantity fluffy icing
● purple and pink (or peach) food colouring ● green, yellow,
pink and white thin marshmallows ● coloured sugar balls
● purple jelly bean, halved, for eyes ● pink heart-shaped
candy, for cheeks ● banana sweet, for mouth ● fried noodles,
for hair ● cardboard wand**

Cut cakes into shapes as shown in diagram below. Divide
icing in half. Tint one portion purple. Reserve 1/3 cup of the
remaining plain icing. Tint the rest pale peach or pink. Ice
cake as shown. Tint a small portion of the pink icing darker,
use to pipe outline of face and body. Use reserved plain icing
for face and hands. Decorate with sweets as shown.

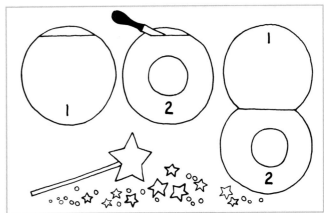

PARTY FOOD

PSYCHEDELIC FAIRY BREAD

Preparation time: 10 minutes *Total cooking time:* Nil
Serves 8

8 slices white bread • 40 g soft butter • coloured sprinkles

1 Spread bread with butter, then remove crusts. Place a biscuit cutter or egg ring on the centre of the slice as a guide. Sprinkle a light coating of one type of sprinkle inside the guide; sprinkle a contrasting type outside the guide.
2 Remove cutter; press in sprinkles gently with fingers.

FAIRY CAKES

Preparation time: 15 minutes *Total cooking time:* 15 minutes
Makes about 35

340 g packet buttercake mix ◆ 2 teaspoons grated lemon rind ◆ 2/3 cup lemon butter ◆ 1/2 cup thickened or pouring cream ◆ silver balls, to decorate ◆ 1/4 cup icing sugar

1 Preheat oven to moderate 180°C. Line two 12-cup deep patty tins with patty cases. Make up cake mixture by following directions on packet. Mix in rind.
2 Place 1 tablespoon batter in each patty case. Bake 15 minutes. Cool on wire rack.
3 When cakes have cooled, cut a round section from the top of each cake, leaving a small cavity in the cake. Cut rounds in half. Place 1/2 teaspoon lemon butter in each cavity. Beat cream until firm peaks form. Spoon 1 tablespoon cream into each cavity. Press half-circles on top to make wing shapes. Decorate with silver balls. Dust with icing sugar.

BAT WINGS: Make cakes as above with chocolate packet mix. To make filling combine 1/2 cup whipped cream with 2 tablespoons chocolate ice-cream topping.

FAIRY WANDS

Preparation time: 20 minutes + 1 hour refrigeration
Total cooking time: 15 minutes per tray *Makes* 10

90 g butter, chopped • 1/3 cup caster sugar • 3/4 cup plain flour • 1/4 cup self-raising flour • 2 tablespoons custard powder • 1 egg, lightly beaten • 200 g dark chocolate melts, melted • 10 coloured icy-pole sticks • coloured balls

1 Place butter, sugar, flours and custard powder in food processor. Process 30 seconds or until mixture is fine and crumbly. Add egg and process 20 seconds or until a soft dough forms. Turn onto floured surface and knead 30 seconds. Cover with plastic wrap and refrigerate 1 hour.
2 Preheat oven to moderate 180°C. Line two oven trays with baking paper. Roll dough out between 2 sheets of baking paper to 3 mm thickness. Cut dough into star shapes using a 9 cm star-shaped cutter. Arrange stars on prepared trays and bake 15 minutes or until lightly golden. Cool on trays. Repeat process with any remaining dough scraps.
3 Place 1/2 teaspoon of melted chocolate on flat side of half of the biscuit; attach stick. Sandwich the remaining biscuits over chocolate and press to secure. Allow chocolate to set.

Here is a selection of sweet and savoury treats to keep little party-goers happy

Dip top of each wand diagonally into chocolate, coating both sides. Sprinkle with coloured balls. Allow to set on baking paper. Alternatively, place chocolate in a paper piping bag and drizzle over wands. Decorate and allow to set.

CHICKEN TOASTS

Preparation time: 10 minutes *Total cooking time:* 15 minutes
Makes 32

1 large chicken breast fillet, chopped ▲ 1 egg ▲ 1/2 teaspoon lemon pepper ▲ 2 spring onions, chopped ▲ 8 slices white bread ▲ 40 g softened butter

1 Preheat oven to moderate 180°C. Line two oven trays with foil. Place chicken, egg, lemon pepper and spring onion in food processor. Process 30 seconds or until smooth.
2 Spread mixture evenly over bread. Cut crusts from bread and cut each slice into 4 triangles. Place on prepared trays. Bake 15 minutes or until golden and slightly puffed.
PRAWN TOASTS: Make as above, substituting 375 g peeled, deveined prawns for chicken.

Left to right: Psychedelic Fairy Bread, Bat Wings and Fairy Cakes, Fairy Wands, Chicken Toasts, Prawn Toasts, Cheese and Bacon Tarts, Cheese and Salmon Tarts

CHEESE AND BACON TARTS

Preparation time: 30 minutes *Total cooking time:* 15 minutes
Makes about 18

2 sheets ready-rolled shortcrust pastry • 2 rashers bacon, finely chopped • 1 small onion, finely chopped • 1/2 cup cream • 1 egg • 1/2 teaspoon mild mustard • 1/2 cup grated cheddar cheese

1 Preheat oven to moderate 180°C. Brush two shallow 12-cup patty tins with melted butter or oil.
2 Lay out pastry on a lightly floured surface. Cut out rounds with a 7 cm fluted cutter. Ease pastry rounds into patty tins. Sprinkle chopped bacon and onion over pastry shells. Combine cream, egg and mustard in small bowl. Whisk until smooth. Spoon 1 teaspoon of mixture into each pastry case. Sprinkle with grated cheese. Bake 15 minutes or until golden and crisp. Serve warm.
CHEESE AND SALMON TARTS: Make as above, substituting 1/3 cup drained and flaked canned salmon for chopped bacon.

ROCKY **ROAD**

Preparation time: 10 minutes *Total cooking time:* 5 minutes
Makes about 36 pieces

$^1/_4$ cup desiccated coconut ♦ 100 g white marshmallows
♦ 100 g pink marshmallows ♦ $^1/_2$ cup mixed, unsalted nuts
♦ $^1/_4$ cup glacé cherries, halved ♦ 375 g dark chocolate melts

1 Line base and sides of a shallow 28 x 18 cm cake tin with
foil. Sprinkle half the coconut over base of the prepared tin.
2 Cut marshmallows in half and arrange in tin alternating
colours and leaving a little space between the pieces. Sprinkle
remaining coconut, nuts and cherries in spaces between
marshmallows and around edge of tin.
3 Place the chocolate in a medium heatproof bowl. Stand
bowl over a pan of simmering water; stir until chocolate has
melted. Cool slightly. Pour over marshmallow mixture. Tap
tin gently on bench to settle chocolate. Leave to set. When
firm, cut into pieces with a sharp knife.

CAVEMEN CLUBS

Preparation time: 10 minutes + 4 hours freezing
Total cooking time: 5 minutes *Makes* 9

3 large bananas, peeled and cut into 3 ● wooden icy-pole
sticks, cut in half ● 125 g dark cooking chocolate, chopped
● 20 g white vegetable shortening (copha) ● $^1/_2$ cup crushed nuts

1 Line a 32 x 28 cm oven tray with foil. Carefully push a
half-stick into each piece of banana. Place on prepared tray
and freeze 2 hours or until firm.
2 Combine chocolate and shortening in a small heatproof
bowl. Stand bowl over pan of simmering water; stir until
chocolate has melted and mixture is smooth.

3 Working with one at a time, dip each whole banana piece
into hot chocolate mixture; drain off excess chocolate. Roll
half of each chocolate-coated banana in crushed nuts. Place
on prepared tray. Refrigerate until chocolate has set, then
wrap in plastic wrap and place in freezer at least 2 hours.
Serve immediately.
FROZEN BANANA BITES: Make as above, omitting
nuts to make plain choc-coated bananas.

SWAMP **MUD**

Preparation time: 20 minutes + 2 hours refrigeration
Total cooking time: Nil *Serves* 8

150 g dark cooking chocolate, chopped ▲ 4 eggs, separated
▲ 2 tablespoons caster sugar ▲ 1 teaspoon grated orange rind
▲ $^1/_3$ cup cream ▲ 1 teaspoon gelatine ▲ 1 tablespoon orange
juice ▲ hundreds and thousands, for topping

1 Place chocolate in a small heatproof bowl. Stand bowl over
a pan of simmering water; stir until chocolate has melted and
mixture is smooth. Cool slightly.
2 Using electric beaters, beat yolks, sugar and rind in a large
bowl 5 minutes or until thick and creamy. Beat in cream and
melted chocolate.
3 Combine gelatine with juice in a small bowl. Stand bowl in
hot water; stir until gelatine dissolves. Add to the chocolate
mixture and beat until combined.
4 Place egg whites in a small bowl. Using electric beaters,
beat until firm peaks form. Add to chocolate mixture. Using
a metal spoon, fold in together until well combined.
Refrigerate 2 hours or until set. Sprinkle with hundreds
and thousands. Can be served with chocolate sticks or
bars, if desired.

Left to right: Rocky Road, Cavemen Clubs and Frozen Banana Bites, Swamp Mud, Baby Burgers, Dinosaur Eggs, Meatballs

DINOSAUR **EGGS**

Preparation time: 30 minutes *Total cooking time:* Nil
Makes 40

1 cup dried apricots, finely chopped ▲ 1 cup desiccated coconut ▲ $1/2$ cup sweetened condensed milk ▲ desiccated coconut, extra

1 In a bowl, combine apricots, coconut and condensed milk; mix well.
2 Roll 2 teaspoons of mixture into a small ball; repeat with remaining mixture. Roll balls in extra desiccated coconut. Refrigerate until set.

MEAT**BALLS**

Preparation time: 15 minutes *Total cooking time:* 10 minutes
Makes about 25

375 g beef mince ■ 1 small onion, finely chopped ■ $1/2$ cup fresh breadcrumbs ■ 1 tablespoon tomato paste ■ 1 teaspoon worcestershire sauce ■ 1 egg, lightly beaten ■ 2 tablespoons oil

1 Place mince, onion, breadcrumbs, tomato paste, sauce and egg in large bowl. Using hands, mix until well combined. Shape level tablespoons of mixture into balls.
2 Heat oil in a large frying pan. Add meatballs and cook over medium heat, shaking pan often, 10 minutes or until meatballs are cooked and evenly browned. Drain on paper towels. Serve hot or cold with tomato sauce, if desired.

BABY BURGERS

Preparation time: 30 minutes *Total cooking time:* 10 minutes
Makes 10

500 g beef mince • 1 small onion, finely chopped
• 1 tablespoon finely chopped parsley • 1 egg, lightly beaten
• 1 tablespoon tomato sauce • $1/2$ teaspoon herb pepper
• 2 tablespoons oil • 10 small bread rolls, halved
• 2 cups finely shredded lettuce • 2 small tomatoes, thinly sliced • 5 rings canned pineapple, drained and halved
• 5 cheese slices, halved • tomato or barbecue sauce

1 Combine mince, onion, parsley, beaten egg, tomato sauce and herb pepper in a large bowl. Using hands, mix until well combined. Divide the mixture into 10 portions. Shape into round patties.
2 Heat oil in a large, heavy-based pan over medium heat. Cook patties 5 minutes each side, or until they are well browned. Remove and drain on paper towels.
3 To assemble burgers place a patty on the base of a roll. Top with lettuce, tomato, pineapple slice and cheese slice. Add sauce and finish with roll top. Serve immediately.

SAUSAGE **ROLLS**

Preparation time: 35 minutes *Total cooking time:* 25 minutes
Makes 48

1 teaspoon oil ● 1 onion, finely chopped ● 500 g sausage
mince ● 1 cup soft white breadcrumbs ● 2 tablespoons
tomato sauce ● 1 egg, lightly beaten ● 3 sheets frozen ready-
rolled puff pastry, thawed ● egg or milk, for glazing

1 Preheat oven to moderately hot 210°C (190°C gas). Lightly
grease an oven tray.
2 Heat oil in frying pan; add onion and cook, over low heat,
until soft and transparent. In a bowl combine onion, mince,
breadcrumbs, tomato sauce and egg.
3 Lay pastry sheets on a lightly floured board and cut into
three, horizontally. Divide the meat mixture into six equal
portions and spoon across the long edge of the pastry. Roll
up to form a long sausage shape. Brush lightly with a little
beaten egg or milk. Cut rolls into 4 cm lengths and place on
prepared tray.
4 Bake 10 minutes; reduce heat to 180°C and bake
15 minutes until rolls are golden. Serve with tomato sauce.
NOTE: Sausage rolls can be frozen for up to 2 weeks before
serving. Thaw and reheat in a moderate oven (180°C)
30 minutes.

CORNY CHEESE **ROW** BOATS

Preparation time: 25 minutes *Total cooking time:* 10 minutes
Makes 24

40 g butter ▲ 1 tablespoon plain flour ▲ $1/2$ cup milk ▲ $1/4$ cup
grated cheddar cheese ▲ $1/4$ teaspoon chicken stock powder
▲ 130 g can corn kernels, drained ▲ herb pepper, to taste
▲ 24 plain vol-au-vent cases ▲ 24 straight pretzels, halved

1 Heat butter in a medium pan; add flour. Stir over low heat
1 minute. Add milk gradually to pan, stirring until smooth.
Stir constantly over medium heat 5 minutes or until the
mixture boils and thickens. Boil 1 minute more; remove
from heat. Stir in cheese, stock powder, corn and pepper.
2 Spoon 3 teaspoons of mixture into each vol-au-vent case.
Arrange pretzels as oars. Serve warm.
MOON MOGULS: Row Boats can become 'Moon
Moguls' for the Outer space party by omitting pretzels.

PIRATE **FACE** BISCUITS

Preparation time: 15 minutes *Total cooking time:* Nil
Makes 30

2 cups icing sugar ● 1–2 tablespoons water ● 250 g large plain
round biscuits ● 2–3 drops yellow food colouring ● 30 small
jellies ● 15 chocolate buds, halved ● 5 snakes, sliced
● 4 licorice straps, chopped ● $1/2$ cup chocolate sprinkles

1 Combine icing sugar and water in small bowl. Stand bowl over pan of simmering water; stir until smooth. Tint with food colouring. Spread biscuits evenly with icing.
2 Make pirate faces while icing is still wet, using jellies for eyes, a half-bud for eye-patch, snake pieces for mouth, licorice portions for scars, and sprinkles for hair. Store in refrigerator until needed.
PUNK FACES: Make hair with green sprinkles and change face's expression to a scowl.

MARTIAN BISCUITS

Preparation time: 15 minutes + 30 minutes refrigeration
Total cooking time: 15 minutes **Makes** 24

125 g butter ▲ ¹/2 cup caster sugar ▲ 1 egg ▲ 1³/4 cups plain flour ▲ 1 cup icing sugar ▲ 3 teaspoons hot water ▲ 4 drops green food colouring ▲ 1 packet licorice allsorts, thinly sliced

1 Using electric beaters, beat butter, sugar and egg in a medium bowl until light and creamy.
2 Add flour to mixture. Using hands, press the mixture together to form a soft dough. Turn onto a lightly floured surface; knead 2 minutes or until smooth. Refrigerate, covered with plastic wrap, 30 minutes.
3 Preheat oven to moderate 180°C. Brush a 32 x 28 cm biscuit tray with melted butter or oil. Roll dough, between sheets of baking paper, to 5 mm thickness. Cut into shapes using an 8 cm gingerbread cutter. Place on prepared tray and bake 15 minutes or until golden. Cool on wire rack.
4 Place icing sugar in medium bowl. Add water and food colouring; stir until well combined. Dip the front of each biscuit into icing, holding them over the bowl to allow excess to drain away. While icing is still soft, decorate with licorice allsorts. Biscuits can be made up to 7 days ahead and stored in an airtight container.

GALACTIC **DISCS**

Preparation time: 10 minutes *Total cooking time:* 5 minutes
Makes 12

12 small, round honeysnap biscuits ■ 12 large, white marshmallows ■ 20 g butter ■ sweets to decorate

1 Line a 12-cup deep patty tin with patty cases. Place a biscuit in each case.
2 Place marshmallows and butter in a small heatproof bowl; stand bowl over pan of simmering water; stir until mixture is smooth.
3 Spoon mixture over biscuits and decorate with clusters of sweets. Refrigerate until set.

SPACE SPUDS

Preparation time: 10 minutes *Total cooking time:* 50 minutes
Makes 12

8 small cocktail potatoes ◆ ¹/4 cup sour cream ◆ 20 g butter ◆ 1 egg ◆ 1 tablespoon mayonnaise ◆ 2 tablespoons chopped chives ◆ 3 bacon rashers, chopped ◆ ¹/2 cup grated cheddar cheese ◆ chives, extra, to garnish

1 Preheat oven to moderate 180°C. Wrap potatoes in foil. Bake 30–40 minutes or until tender.
2 Cut potatoes in half; spoon out flesh, leaving a thick shell. Reserve flesh. Combine sour cream, butter, egg, mayonnaise, chives, bacon and reserved potato flesh in a small bowl; mix well. Spoon mixture into potato skins. Place potatoes on an oven tray.
3 Sprinkle with cheese and bake 10 minutes or until cheese has melted. Garnish with extra chives.

Left to right: Sausage Rolls, Corny Cheese Row Boats and Moon Moguls, Pirate Face Biscuits, Martian Biscuits, Galactic Discs, Space Spuds

47

ROCK **CAKES**

Preparation time: 10 minutes *Total cooking time:* 15 minutes
Makes 18

2 cups self-raising flour ▲ 1 teaspoon mixed spice
▲ 90 g butter, chopped ▲ 1/2 cup sugar ▲ 1/4 cup sultanas
▲ 2 tablespoons mixed peel ▲ 1 egg ▲ 1/3 cup milk
▲ 1/4 cup sugar, extra

1 Preheat oven to moderate 180°C. Line two oven trays with
baking paper. Sift flour and spice into a bowl. Add sugar and
butter. Rub in butter until it resembles coarse breadcrumbs.
2 Mix in sultanas and mixed peel. Make a well in the centre.
Add combined egg and milk and mix to form a soft dough.
3 Drop tablespoonsful of dough onto prepared trays, allowing
room for spreading. Sprinkle lightly with extra sugar and
bake 10–15 minutes or until golden.

UFOS

Preparation time: 20 minutes + 30 minutes refrigeration
Total cooking time: 20 minutes *Makes* 24

1/2 cup plain flour ◆ 40 g butter, chopped ◆ 1 tablespoon
sugar ◆ 1 tablespoon water ◆ 2 tablespoons custard powder
◆ 1 tablespoon sugar, extra ◆ 3/4 cup milk ◆ 12 small
strawberries, halved ◆ 2 tablespoons apple gel (see Note)

1 Grease two 12-cup shallow patty tins. Sift flour into a
bowl; add butter. Using fingertips, rub butter into flour until
mixture is fine and crumbly. Add sugar; mix. Add almost all
the water and mix to a firm dough, adding more water if

necessary. Turn dough out onto lightly floured surface and
knead 2 minutes until smooth. Refrigerate dough, covered
with plastic wrap, 30 minutes.
2 Preheat oven to moderate 180°C. Roll pastry out, between
sheets of baking paper, to 2 mm thickness and cut into
rounds using a 5 cm cutter. Press rounds into prepared tins.
Bake 15 minutes until golden; cool.
3 Combine custard powder and sugar in small pan; add
enough of the milk to make a smooth paste. Add remaining
milk; stir over low heat until mixture boils and thickens. Set
custard aside to cool. When cool, place a teaspoon of custard
into each pastry case. Top with strawberry half and brush
with warmed apple gel.
NOTE: Apple gel is available from the baby-food section of
the supermarket.

METEOR ICE-CREAM **CONES**

Preparation time: 20 minutes *Total cooking time:* 5 minutes
Makes 8

500 ml vanilla ice-cream ● 8 round flat-based ice-cream
cones ● 200 g small jubes, to decorate ● 150 g dark chocolate
melts, melted

1 Place 2 scoops of ice-cream into each cone, packing it
down firmly. Press jubes into ice-cream. Place cones in
freezer for 10 minutes to re-harden ice-cream. Working with

one cone at a time, carefully dip the ice-cream into melted chocolate. Drain excess chocolate. Allow to set.

TOADSTOOLS: Pack cones with ice-cream and place in freezer for 10 minutes. Carefully dip one cone at a time into melted chocolate; drain off excess. While chocolate is still warm press Smarties into chocolate. Allow to set.

CHOC-CHIP CRACKLES

Preparation time: 20 minutes *Total cooking time:* 5 minutes
Makes 24

3 cups Rice Bubbles ■ ¹/4 cup cocoa powder ■ 1¹/4 cups icing sugar ■ ¹/2 cup sultanas ■ ³/4 cup desiccated coconut ■ 200 g white vegetable shortening (copha), melted ■ ¹/3 cup dark choc bits

1 Line two deep 12-cup patty tins with silver-foil patty cases. Combine Rice Bubbles, cocoa and sugar in large bowl; mix thoroughly, then stir in sultanas and coconut. Stir in melted shortening.
2 Spoon mixture into prepared patty tins. Sprinkle with choc bits. Allow to set.

BANANA, NUT AND DATE FINGERS

Preparation time: 10 minutes *Total cooking time:* Nil
Makes 18

20 g butter ♦ 12 slices white bread ♦ 3 medium bananas, mashed ♦ 6 fresh dates, chopped ♦ ¹/4 cup crushed nuts

1 Butter bread.
2 Spread 6 slices with mashed banana and top with dates and nuts. Top with remaining bread.
3 Remove crusts with sharp knife and cut each sandwich into 3 fingers.

Left to right: Rock Cakes, UFOs, Choc-chip Crackles, Meteor Ice-cream Cones and Toadstools, Banana, Nut and Date Fingers, Camel Humps, Desert Sand and Star Dust

CAMEL HUMPS

Preparation time: 15 minutes *Total cooking time:* Nil
Makes 10

200 g caramel buds, melted ● 10 milk arrowroot biscuits ● 20 small white marshmallows ● ³/4 cup desiccated coconut

1 Spread a small amount of caramel on each biscuit. Before caramel sets, place two marshmallows, side by side, on each biscuit. Allow to set.
2 Dip biscuits into remaining caramel to coat marshmallows and tops of biscuits. Sprinkle with coconut; allow to set.

DESERT SAND

Preparation time: 15 minutes *Total cooking time:* Nil
Serves 10

3 cups icing sugar ■ 1 teaspoon yellow food colour ■ 2 x 25 g packets Fruit Tingles ■ ¹/4 teaspoon bicarbonate of soda

1 Place sugar in a large freezer bag; add a few drops of food colouring and shake bag vigorously until sugar is evenly coloured. Transfer to a large bowl.
2 Place Fruit Tingles in food processor and process until finely chopped. Add to icing sugar with soda; mix well.
STAR DUST: Make as above, substituting pink food colouring for yellow.

MINI **PIZZAS**

Preparation time: 40 minutes *Total cooking time:* 10 minutes
Makes 40

2 cups self-raising flour ■ 100 g butter, chopped ■ $1/2$ cup
buttermilk ■ 2 tablespoons tomato paste ■ 1 stick cabanossi,
thinly sliced ■ 1 small onion, thinly sliced ■ 10 cherry
tomatoes, thinly sliced ■ 6 cheese slices, cut into 3 cm rounds

1 Preheat oven to moderate 180°C. Line two 32 x 28 cm
oven trays with foil. Brush with melted butter or oil.
2 Combine flour and butter in food processor. Process
30 seconds or until mixture is a fine crumbly texture. Add
buttermilk; process 30 seconds or until the mixture comes
together. Knead dough gently on a lightly floured surface
until smooth. Roll dough out to 3 mm thick. Cut into
rounds using a 5 cm cutter. Place rounds on prepared tray.
3 Spread rounds with tomato paste. Arrange cabanossi, onion
and tomato on top and sprinkle with cheese. Bake for 10
minutes or until crisp. Garnish with oregano leaf, if desired.

ANIMAL CRISPS

Preparation time: 10 minutes *Total cooking time:* 15 minutes
Makes 20

1 sheet ready-rolled puff pastry ♦ 1 egg, lightly beaten
♦ $1/4$ cup grated cheddar cheese ♦ 1 tablespoon poppy seeds
♦ 1 tablespoon onion flakes

1 Preheat oven to moderate 180°C. Line an oven tray with
baking paper. Cut animal shapes out of pastry using assorted
biscuit cutters. Place on prepared tray. Brush with egg.
Sprinkle shapes with combined cheese, poppy seeds and
onion flakes. Bake 10–15 minutes or until golden crisp.
STARRY NIGHT CRISPS: Cut puff pastry into
star and moon shapes with a knife
or biscuit cutters.

CHICKEN **NUGGETS**

Preparation time: 20 minutes *Total cooking time:* 15 minutes
Makes 34

375 g chicken thigh fillets, roughly chopped ● 1 egg
● 1 tablespoon chopped fresh chives ● $1/4$ teaspoon sesame oil
● 2 teaspoons plum sauce ● 1 teaspoon soy sauce
● 1 cup cornflakes

1 Preheat oven to moderate 180°C. Line a 32 x 28 cm oven
tray with foil. Brush with melted butter or oil.
2 Place chicken, egg, chives, sesame oil and sauces in food
processor. Process 30 seconds or until mixture is smooth.
3 Shape heaped teaspoons of mixture into balls. Roll balls in
cornflakes. Place nuggets on prepared tray. Bake
15 minutes or until golden and crisp.

ZEBRA SANDWICHES

Preparation time: 10 minutes *Total cooking time:* Nil
Makes 8

4 slices white bread ▲ 20 g butter ▲ 1 tablespoon Vegemite
(yeast extract) or hazelnut spread

1 Spread 3 slices of bread with butter and either Vegemite or
hazelnut spread. Stack slices, spread side up. Top with the
unbuttered slice. Press down gently.
2 Using a sharp knife, cut crusts neatly from bread. Cut the
stack in half to make rectangles, then slice each rectangle
crossways into four fingers.
HINT: Use animal shaped biscuit cutters to cut out
sandwiches, if desired.

CHOCOLATE **HAYSTACKS**

Preparation time: 30 minutes *Total cooking time:* 10 minutes
Makes 40

2 cups sugar ■ ¹/3 cup cocoa powder ■ ¹/2 cup milk
■ 125 g butter, chopped ■ 3 cups rolled oats
■ 1¹/2 cups shredded coconut

1 Combine sugar and cocoa in a large heavy-based pan. Add milk and butter. Stir over low heat, without boiling, until butter has melted and sugar has completely dissolved. Bring mixture to the boil, stirring constantly; remove from heat immediately. Add the rolled oats and shredded coconut; stir until well combined.
2 Working quickly, drop heaped teaspoons of chocolate mixture onto greaseproof paper. Allow to set. Store in an airtight container in a cool, dry place until ready to use.
HINT: For easier handling, spoon the hot chocolate mixture into paper patty cases.

FRUIT **JELLY** SHAPES

Preparation time: 15 minutes + overnight refrigeration
Total cooking time: 5 minutes *Serves* 6–8

2 cups orange juice ▲ 2 tablespoons sugar ▲ ¹/4 cup gelatine

1 Line base and sides of an 18 x 28 cm cake tin with aluminium foil. Brush with oil.
2 Combine juice and sugar in medium heavy-based pan. Sprinkle gelatine over syrup.

Stir over low heat, without boiling, until sugar and gelatine have completely dissolved. Bring to boil; boil 1 minute. Remove from heat immediately. Pour mixture into the prepared tin, straining if lumpy. Refrigerate overnight.
3 Turn jelly out of tin. Cut into a variety of shapes using biscuit cutters. Refrigerate shapes until ready to serve.
HINT: For a bright and colourful display, make two or three Fruit Jelly Shapes; try lime, orange and blackcurrant juices.

ANIMAL **FEED**

Preparation time: 5 minutes *Total cooking time:* Nil
Serves 10

1 cup plain or assorted rice crackers ● 1 cup banana crisps
● 1 cup shredded or flaked coconut ● 1 cup sultanas
● 1 cup raisins ● 2 cups toasted muesli ● 4 cups fresh popcorn
● 1 cup sunflower kernels, pumpkin seeds or pepitas (peeled pumpkin seeds)

1 Combine all ingredients in a large bowl and mix well. Spoon into individual bags as a take-home treat or place in containers for serving.

Left to right: Mini Pizzas, Starry Night Crisps, Animal Crisps, Chicken Nuggets, Zebra Sandwiches, Chocolate Haystacks, Fruit Jelly Shapes, Animal Feed

FISH COCKTAILS

Preparation time: 20 minutes
Total cooking time: 15 minutes *Makes* 24

250 g boneless white fish fillets ▲ 2 tablespoons plain flour ▲ 1 egg white ▲ ¼ cup cornflake crumbs ▲ mayonnaise

1 Preheat oven to moderate 180°C. Cut fish into pieces about 3 cm square. Coat fish pieces in flour; shake off excess.
2 Whisk egg white in small bowl. Dip fish, one piece at a time, in egg white; coat with cornflake crumbs. Place in a single layer on oven tray. Bake 15 minutes or until golden; turn pieces over after 10 minutes. Serve hot with mayonnaise.

LIFESAVERS

Preparation time: 25 minutes *Total cooking time:* 30 minutes *Makes* 5

2 egg whites ■ ½ cup caster sugar ■ ¼ cup thickened or pouring cream, whipped ■ raspberry jam, for spreading ■ fine red ribbon

1 Preheat oven to slow 150°C. Line two oven trays with baking paper. Use a plate to draw five 5 cm circles on each sheet of paper.
2 Beat egg whites with electric beaters until stiff peaks form. Add sugar, a tablespoon at a time, beating well after each addition. Beat until mixture is thick and glossy, and sugar has dissolved. Place meringue in a piping bag fitted with a plain nozzle. Pipe around inside edge of marked circles only. Bake 20–30 minutes or until meringue is pale and dry. Turn oven off; cool meringues in oven with door ajar.
3 Near serving time, sandwich two meringues together with jam and cream. Thread ribbon through centre and tie a bow.

Left to right: Fish Cocktails, Lifesavers, Sunken Subs, Fishermen's Burgers, Speckled Bubble Bars, Popcorn Pearls, Sunburst Parfait

SUNKEN SUBS

Preparation time: 10 minutes *Total cooking time:* 15 minutes *Makes* 8

4 hot dog rolls ◆ 20 g butter ◆ 1 clove garlic, crushed ◆ 440 g can spaghetti in tomato and cheese sauce ◆ 80 g sliced ham, chopped ◆ 100 g cheddar cheese slices, cut into strips

1 Preheat oven to moderate 180°C. Lightly grease an oven tray. Cut rolls in half horizontally; place on prepared tray.
2 Heat butter in pan; add garlic and cook 2–3 minutes. Brush a little on each roll half; top with spaghetti, ham and cheese. Bake 12 minutes or until cheese melts and bread is crispy.

FISHERMEN'S BURGERS

Preparation time: 15 minutes *Total cooking time:* 15 minutes *Makes* 6

6 fish fingers ● 3 rashers bacon, cut in half ● 6 small lettuce leaves ● 6 small dinner rolls, halved ● 3 cheese slices, cut in half ● 6 teaspoons mayonnaise

1 Preheat oven to moderate 180°C. Wrap each fish finger in a piece of bacon. Place on oven tray and bake 15 minutes.
2 To assemble burgers place a lettuce leaf on the base of each roll. Top with cheese, fish finger, then a teaspoon of mayonnaise. Finish with roll top.

SPECKLED BUBBLE BARS

Preparation time: 20 minutes + 1–2 hours setting
Total cooking time: 5 minutes *Makes* 24

1¹/2 cups marshmallows ▲ 60 g butter ▲ 2¹/2 cups Rice Bubbles ▲ ¹/2 cup hundreds and thousands

1 Line an 18 x 28 cm shallow tin with foil or baking paper; grease lightly. Place marshmallows and butter in pan. Stir over low heat until both have melted. Remove from heat.
2 Place Rice Bubbles and hundreds and thousands in a large bowl. Pour in marshmallow mixture and mix well.
3 Pour mixture into prepared tin; smooth surface. Allow to cool and set. When cool, cut into bars.

POPCORN PEARLS

Preparation time: 1 hour *Total cooking time:* 30 minutes
Serves 10

¹/3 cup vegetable oil • 1 cup popping corn • 1 cup white sugar
• 1 tablespoon honey • 1 tablespoon golden syrup
• ¹/2 cup water • 60 g butter

1 Heat oil in large pan; add popping corn and cover pan with a lid. Cook over medium heat, shaking pan occasionally. When popping stops, take off lid and transfer popcorn to a large bowl, discarding any unpopped corn.
2 Combine sugar, honey, golden syrup, water and butter in a heavy-based pan and bring slowly to the boil, stirring until the sugar dissolves. Wash undissolved crystals down sides of pan with a wet pastry brush. Ensure all the sugar dissolves

before mixture boils. Boil until mixture reaches 150°C on a sugar thermometer. If you have no thermometer, test by dropping a small amount of mixture in iced water—it should turn hard and brittle.

3 Pour toffee over popcorn and mix until well coated. Continue stirring until mixture sets and cools slightly. Place on large tray to cool. Cut twelve 50 cm lengths of heavy cotton. Using a thick needle, thread pieces of popcorn onto cotton to make necklaces. Tie ends of cotton together.

SUNBURST PARFAIT

Preparation time: 30 minutes + 1 hour refrigeration
Total cooking time: 5 minutes *Makes* 6

■ 2 tablespoons custard powder ■ ¹/4 cup caster sugar
■ 1¹/2 cups milk ■ ¹/2 cup cream ■ 1 egg yolk ■ 1 teaspoon vanilla essence ■ 1 packet orange or apricot jelly crystals
■ 2 cups boiling water ■ 1 cup (200 g) canned apricots, sliced
■ whipped cream and orange and kiwi fruit pieces, to serve

1 Combine custard powder and sugar in a medium heavy-based pan. Gradually whisk in the combined milk and cream. Stir, over low heat, 5 minutes or until mixture boils and thickens. Remove from heat. Whisk in yolk and essence. Pour custard into goblets. Refrigerate until firm.
2 Combine jelly crystals and water in a jug. Stir until all crystals have dissolved. Set aside until jelly reaches room temperature.
3 Arrange apricot slices over custard; top with cooled jelly and refrigerate to set. Just before serving, decorate with whipped cream and fruit.

BEACH BABY JELLIES

Preparation time: 20 minutes + overnight refrigeration
Total cooking time: Nil **Makes** 12

**85 g packet green jelly crystals ● 2 cups boiling water
● 2 tablespoons fine biscuit crumbs ● 12 jelly babies
● 12 Lifesavers ● 12 paper parasols**

1 Line a 12-cup patty tin with two layers of paper patty cases.
2 Combine jelly crystals and water in a jug. Stir until all the crystals have dissolved. Set aside until cool. Pour jelly into patty cases to three-quarters full. Refrigerate overnight.
3 Sprinkle biscuit crumbs over half of each jelly. Lay a jelly baby on the crumbs. Place a Lifesaver on other half of jelly and put a paper parasol through the centre.

HAM AND PINEAPPLE PINWHEELS

Preparation time: 25 minutes *Total cooking time:* 15 minutes
Makes about 30

**2 sheets ready-rolled puff pastry ■ 1 egg, lightly beaten
■ 100 g ham, thinly sliced ■ 150 g can crushed pineapple,
well drained ■ 1/3 cup grated cheddar cheese**

1 Preheat oven to moderate 180°C. Line two 32 x 28 cm oven trays with aluminium foil. Brush trays with melted butter or oil.
2 Lay out pastry sheets, brush with beaten egg. Sprinkle evenly with ham, pineapple and cheese. Press gently onto the pastry.
3 Roll up each sheet of pastry firmly. Using a sharp flat-bladed or electric knife, cut each roll into 10 rounds. Place pinwheels on prepared trays allowing room for spreading. Bake 15 minutes or until golden and puffed. Serve warm.

*Left to right: Beach Baby Jellies, Ham and
Pineapple Pinwheels, Frosted Brownies and
Crunchy Top Brownies, Coconut Ice, Snowmen*

FROSTED BROWNIES

Preparation time: 35 minutes *Total cooking time:* 30 minutes
Makes about 25

**1 cup plain flour ● 1/2 cup cocoa powder ● 1/2 teaspoon
baking powder ● 1/4 teaspoon salt ● 125 g butter, softened
● 11/2 cups soft brown sugar ● 3 eggs ● 1 teaspoon vanilla
essence ● 1/2 cup unsalted peanuts, chopped ● 60 g butter
● 1 cup icing sugar, sifted ● 1/4 cup peanut butter
● 1 tablespoon boiling water**

1 Preheat oven to moderate 180°C. Grease a 28 x 18 cm shallow baking tin. Sift flour, cocoa, baking powder and salt into a bowl. Using electric beaters, beat butter and sugar in a separate bowl until light and creamy. Add eggs and vanilla; beat well. Using a metal spoon, fold in sifted dry ingredients and peanuts; combine thoroughly.
2 Spoon mixture into prepared tin. Bake 30 minutes or until skewer comes out clean when inserted in the centre. Cool brownies in tin. When cold, spread with frosting.
3 Beat butter and icing sugar until creamy. Combine peanut butter with water and beat into mixture until smooth. Spread evenly over brownies.

CRUNCHY TOP BROWNIES: Make brownie bases as above. Omit peanut butter in topping and substitute 2 tablespoons cocoa powder. Sprinkle iced brownies with 1/3 cup Cocoa Pops.

COCONUT ICE

Preparation time: 30 minutes + 1 hour refrigeration
Total cooking time: Nil *Makes* 30 pieces

2¹/₂ cups icing sugar ▲ ¹/₄ teaspoon cream of tartar
▲ 1 egg white, lightly beaten ▲ ¹/₄ cup condensed milk
▲ 1³/₄ cups desiccated coconut ▲ pink food colouring

1 Brush a 26 x 8 x 4.5 cm bar tin with melted butter or oil.
Line the base with baking paper; grease paper.
2 Sift icing sugar and cream of tartar into bowl; make a well
in the centre. Add combined egg white and condensed milk.
Using a wooden spoon, stir in half the coconut. Add the
remaining coconut. Mix until well combined. Divide the
mixture between two bowls. Tint contents of one bowl with
pink colouring. Knead colour through evenly.
3 Press pink mixture over base of prepared tin; cover with
the white mixture and press down gently. Refrigerate 1 hour
or until set. When firm, remove from tin and cut into
squares. Coconut Ice can be stored in an airtight container in
a cool dark place for up to 2 weeks.

SNOWMEN

Preparation time: 30 minutes + 30 minutes freezing
Total cooking time: Nil *Makes* 10

2 litres vanilla ice-cream • 10 pink marshmallows
• ³/₄ cup desiccated coconut • 10 thin strips of licorice
• 20 Smarties • 4 red glacé cherries, cut into quarters

1 Using a large ice-cream scoop, place 10 scoops of ice-
cream on a flat tray. Make 10 more scoops using a smaller
scoop. Place these on large scoops. Freeze 30 minutes to
become very firm. Slice marshmallows into hat shapes.
2 Remove ice-cream from freezer, roll in coconut and top
each with a marshmallow. Tie licorice around neck to form a
scarf. Use Smarties for eyes; make a mouth with glacé cherry
piece. Return to freezer until ready to serve.

Left to right: Guacamole and Corn Chips, Kids' Style Nachos, Potato Wedges, Corn Cobs with Butter, Scary Face Pikelets and Cheeky Face Pikelets, Mouse Traps, Frozen Goo

CORN COBS WITH BUTTER

Preparation time: 5 minutes *Total cooking time:* 10 minutes
Serves 10

5 cobs corn ■ 125 g butter ■ salt and cracked pepper, to taste

1 Peel away green husk from corn cobs and remove silk. Cut cobs in half. Place corn in a large pan of cold water, with a few corn husks. Bring to boil and cook 8-10 minutes or until corn is tender.
2 Drain corn; place 1–2 teaspoons butter on each piece. Season with salt and pepper.

KIDS' STYLE NACHOS

Preparation time: 15 minutes *Total cooking time:* 10 minutes
Serves 6–8

210 g red kidney beans, rinsed and drained ▲ 150 g corn chips ▲ 1 cup grated cheddar cheese ▲ 2 medium tomatoes, finely chopped ▲ 2 tablespoons finely chopped spring onions

1 Preheat oven to moderate 180°C. Line a baking tray with foil.
2 Arrange corn chips in a single layer on prepared tray. Sprinkle with cheese, kidney beans and tomatoes. Bake 10 minutes or until the cheese has melted and turned golden. Top with spring onion. Cool slightly before serving.

GUACAMOLE AND CORN CHIPS

Preparation time: 10 minutes *Total cooking time:* Nil
Serves 10

2 ripe avocados ●2–3 tablespoons lemon juice ●1 clove garlic, crushed ●1/2 onion, finely grated ●2 small tomatoes, finely chopped ●1/2 cup sour cream ●few drops Tabasco sauce ●100 g corn chips

1 Mash avocados until smooth. Stir in lemon juice, garlic, onion, tomatoes, sour cream and sauce. Spoon into serving bowl and serve with corn chips.

POTATO WEDGES

Preparation time: 10 minutes *Total cooking time:* 20 minutes
Serves 10

8 large potatoes ♦ 1 tablespoon oil ♦ 1 teaspoon seasoned salt

1 Preheat oven to moderately hot 210°C (190°C gas). Brush a shallow baking tray with oil. Cut each potato into 6–8 wedges. Place on prepared tray. Brush potatoes with oil and sprinkle with salt. Bake 20 minutes or until golden brown.

SCARY FACE PIKELETS

Preparation time: 20 minutes *Total cooking time:* 30 minutes
Makes 24

**220 g packet pikelet mix ● 60 g dark chocolate, chopped
● 50 g butter**

1 Prepare pikelet batter according to instructions on packet.
Leave the mixture to stand 10 minutes.
2 Place chocolate in a small heatproof bowl. Stand bowl over
a pan of simmering water. Stir until chocolate has melted and
mixture is smooth. Spoon chocolate into a small paper icing
bag (see Note); seal open end and snip off tip.
3 Heat a small amount of butter, over medium heat, in a
large, non-stick frying pan. Pipe a small scary face with
chocolate mixture on the base of the pan. Carefully, spoon a
tablespoon of pikelet batter over the face. Cook until bubbles
appear on the surface. (This will be about 30 seconds.) Turn
and cook other side.
4 Remove from pan; repeat with remaining chocolate and
pikelet mixture. Serve warm or cold.
NOTE: To make a paper icing bag cut out a 25 cm square of
greaseproof or baking paper. Fold in half to make a triangle.
Roll up paper to make a cone; fold down the long end and
tuck inside cone. Snip small tip off other end.
CHEEKY FACE PIKELETS: Pipe happy clown faces
with chocolate for the Circus party.

MOUSE TRAPS

Preparation time: 15 minutes *Total cooking time:* 5 minutes
Makes 10

**10 slices bread ▲ 60 g butter, softened ▲ 10 slices sandwich ham
▲ 250 g cheddar cheese, finely grated ▲ 1/4 cup tomato sauce**

1 Preheat grill to high. Toast bread lightly on both sides;
spread one side thinly with butter. Place a slice of ham on
each piece of bread and sprinkle with grated cheese. Spoon 2
teaspoons of tomato sauce in the centre of the bread.
2 Place bread under preheated grill and cook 1–2 minutes
or until cheese melts and tomato sauce spreads slightly.
Serve hot.

FROZEN GOO

Preparation time: 30 minutes + 6 hours freezing
Total cooking time: Nil *Serves* 10

**1 litre vanilla ice-cream ■ 50 g choc bits or chopped
chocolate ■ 1/4 cup chocolate-flavoured syrup ■ 250 g punnet
strawberries, hulled and chopped ■ 1/4 cup strawberry-
flavoured syrup ■ 100 g pink and white marshmallows
■ 8 wooden icy-pole sticks**

1 Soften ice-cream at room temperature until soft but still
quite frozen; divide between 3 large bowls. Mix chocolate
and chocolate syrup into the first portion. Spoon chocolate
mixture into 8 waxed paper cups. Place cups in freezer.
2 Add strawberries and strawberry syrup to second portion.
Spoon evenly on top of the chocolate mixture. Return cups
to freezer for 2–3 hours or until firm.
3 Mix marshmallows into remaining ice-cream portion.
Spoon onto strawberry and chocolate mixture. Insert an icy-
pole stick through all three layers and freeze for a minimum
of three hours to set firm. Peel waxed cups away from ice-
cream when ready to serve.

SQUELCH **AND** CRUNCH

Preparation time: 20 minutes *Total cooking time:* 5 minutes
Makes 20

185 g chocolate biscuits ● $^1/_2$ cup sugar ● 2 teaspoons gelatine
● $^1/_2$ cup water ● 1 teaspoon vanilla essence ● 2–3 drops green
food colouring ● silver balls, to decorate

1 Line two oven trays with foil. Place biscuits on trays.
2 Combine sugar, gelatine and water in pan. Stir, over
medium heat, until sugar dissolves and mixture comes to the
boil. Simmer, without stirring, 4 minutes. Remove from heat
and cool. Using electric beaters, beat syrup 5–6 minutes until
mixture is thick and glossy and has doubled in volume.
3 Add essence and colouring; beat well until there is no
visible streaking. Spread a small amount on each biscuit.
Smooth surface and sprinkle with silver balls.

BLEEDING **FINGERS**

Preparation time: 20 minutes *Total cooking time:* 1 hour
Makes 20

2 egg whites ▲ $^1/_2$ cup sugar ▲ 1 cup desiccated coconut
▲ $^1/_2$ cup raspberry or strawberry jam ▲ 10 coloured
jellybeans

1 Preheat oven to slow 150°C. Line a baking tray with
baking paper; grease paper and dust liberally with cornflour.
2 Beat egg whites until stiff peaks form. Beat in sugar, one
tablespoon at a time, and continue beating until mixture
becomes thick and glossy. Fold through coconut. Fill a piping
bag fitted with a plain 2 cm nozzle with the meringue
mixture. Pipe 8 cm lengths onto prepared tray.
3 Bake in oven 5 minutes; reduce heat to very slow 120°C
and cook a further 45–50 minutes or until meringues are light
and crisp. Turn off oven and leave meringues to cool.
4 In a pan, heat jam over low heat until thin and runny. Pour
into bowl. Cut one end from each jellybean; discard end. Cut
remaining jellybean in half lengthways. Press jellybean on the
end of each meringue. Dip fingertip in warm jam to serve.

BLOOD BATHS

Preparation time: 20 minutes *Total cooking time:* 15 minutes
Makes 12

300 g frozen raspberries ■ 3 sheets ready-rolled puff pastry
■ $^1/_4$ cup icing sugar, sifted

1 Place raspberries in a medium bowl. Allow to stand 10–15
minutes or until thawed slightly. Refrigerate. Preheat oven to
moderate 180°C. Brush a 12-cup $^1/_3$-cup capacity muffin tin
with melted butter or oil. Cut sheets of pastry into 4 equal
squares, line carefully each individual muffin cup.
2 Bake 15 minutes or until golden. Place on a wire rack to
cool and allow puff pastry to settle. Using the back of a
spoon, carefully push down the centre to form a cup.
3 Combine semi-frozen raspberries and icing sugar in a food
processor and process until smooth. Pour the thick raspberry
mixture into cooled pastry cases before serving.

CLOWN **FACES**

Preparation time: 20 minutes *Total cooking time:* Nil
Serves 10

1 litre vanilla ice-cream ◆ 10 square-based ice-cream cones
◆ $^1/_2$ cup shredded coconut ◆ 20 Smarties ◆ 10 glacé cherries
◆ 1 licorice strap, chopped ◆ 5 small red and green snakes

1 Scoop ice-cream into cones; pack down firmly. Sprinkle
top part of ice-cream with coconut to resemble hair. Make
clown eyes with Smarties and licorice pieces. Use a glacé
cherry (or Smartie) for the nose. Cut snakes into small
pieces and use to make mouths.

CHERRY **CRUNCH**

Preparation time: 15 minutes *Total cooking time:* 10 minutes
Makes 20

30 g butter • 2 tablespoons honey • 2 tablespoons soft brown
sugar • 2 cups cornflakes • ¹/₂ cup chopped glacé cherries (100 g)

1 Preheat oven to moderate 180°C. Line 30 deep patty tins
with paper cases.
2 Place butter, honey and sugar in a small pan. Heat gently
until frothy. Combine cornflakes and cherries in a large bowl.
Stir in butter mixture and mix well.
3 Spoon into paper cases. Refrigerate until firm.

CARAMEL POPCORN **BALLS**

Preparation time: 20 minutes *Total cooking time:* 10 minutes
Makes 50 balls

2 tablespoons oil ■ ¹/₂ cup popping corn ■ ³/₄ cup sugar
■ 80 g butter ■ 2 tablespoons honey ■ 2 tablespoons
pouring cream

1 Heat oil in large pan over medium heat. Add popping corn
and cover tightly with lid. Cook 5 minutes or until popping
stops, shaking occasionally. Transfer popcorn to a large bowl;
set aside.
2 Combine sugar, butter, honey and cream in small
heavy-based pan. Stir over medium heat, without boiling,
until the sugar has completely dissolved. Brush sugar crystals

from sides of pan with a wet pastry brush. Bring mixture to
the boil and boil, without stirring, 5 minutes.
3 Pour sugar syrup over popcorn. Using 2 metal spoons,
combine thoroughly with the popcorn. When mixture has
cooled enough to handle, form popcorn into small balls with
oiled hands. Place on wire rack to set. Popcorn balls can be
stored in an airtight container in a cool dark place for up
to a week.

FRANKFURT **BONBONS**

Preparation time: 20 minutes *Total cooking time:* 15 minutes
Makes 12

12 small cocktail frankfurts ▲ 3 sheets ready-rolled puff
pastry ▲ 1 egg, lightly beaten ▲ cotton or jute string

1 Preheat oven to moderate 180°C. Line two 32 x 28 cm
oven trays with aluminium foil. Brush with melted butter or
oil.
2 Prick frankfurts with a fork. Cut each pastry sheet into 4
squares. Brush each square with beaten egg. Place a frankfurt
on each pastry square and roll up; gently press edges together.
3 Carefully pinch in the ends of the pastry. Tie ends loosely
with pieces of string. Cut a fringe in ends, using scissors.
4 Place pastries on the prepared trays; brush lightly with
beaten egg. Bake 15 minutes or until golden.

*Left to right: Squelch and Crunch, Bleeding Fingers,
Blood Baths, Clown Faces, Caramel Popcorn Balls,
Cherry Crunch, Frankfurt Bonbons*

SMALL TOFFEES

Preparation time: 10 minutes *Total cooking time:*
25 minutes *Makes* about 24

4 cups sugar ■ 1 cup water ■ 1 tablespoon vinegar
■ hundreds and thousands or desiccated coconut

1 Line two deep 12-cup patty tins with paper patty cases.
2 Combine sugar, water and vinegar in large heavy-based
pan. Stir over medium heat until sugar has completely
dissolved; do not boil. Brush sugar crystals from sides of pan
with a wet pastry brush. Bring to the boil; reduce heat
slightly. Boil, without stirring, 20 minutes; OR boil until a
teaspoon of mixture dropped into cold water reaches small-
crack stage OR if using a sugar thermometer, boil toffee until
it reaches 138°C. Remove from heat immediately.
3 Pour into patty cases and decorate with hundreds and
thousands or coconut. Leave to set at room temperature.

BUGS IN RUGS

Preparation time: 20 minutes *Total cooking time:* 15 minutes
Makes 12

12 cocktail frankfurts ♦ 3 slices white bread, crusts removed
♦ ¼ cup melted butter ♦ 2 tablespoons poppy seeds

1 Preheat oven to moderate 180°C. Pierce frankfurts all over
with a fork. Cut each slice of bread into quarters. Place a
frankfurt across each piece. Bring up edges and secure with a
toothpick. Brush with butter and sprinkle with poppy seeds.
2 Place on an oven tray; bake 10–15 minutes until bread is
crisp and brown. Remove from oven; serve immediately.
(Remove toothpicks before serving to young children.)

INSY WINSY SPIDERS

Preparation time: 40 minutes *Total cooking
time:* 15 minutes *Makes* 24

340 g packet chocolate cake mix ● 100 g dark chocolate
● 30 g butter ● 4 licorice straps ● 24 red Smarties
● grated chocolate

1 Preheat oven to temperature recommended on the cake-
mix packet. Grease 24 shallow patty tins. Make up cake mix
according to the directions on the packet. Fill each patty cup
two-thirds full with cake mixture. Bake 10–15 minutes or
until cooked. Cool on a wire rack; place a clean oven tray
under rack.
2 Combine chocolate and butter in a small heatproof bowl;
stand bowl over pan of simmering water until chocolate and
butter have melted and mixture is smooth. Remove from
heat and mix well.
3 Spoon chocolate over cakes, ensuring that each cake is
completely covered. The excess that drips onto the tray
underneath can be re-melted and used to pour over cakes, if
necessary. Allow chocolate to set.
4 Cut licorice straps into thin lengths 3 cm long. Attach
eight of these lengths to each cake as spiders' legs. Cut
Smarties in half and place on spiders to represent eyes.
Sprinkle cakes with grated chocolate to make furry bodies.

Left to right: Small Toffees, Bugs in Rugs, Insy Winsy Spiders, Sausage Sizzle, Onion Dip, Cheese Swags

SAUSAGE **SIZZLE**

Preparation time: 50 minutes *Total cooking time:* 20 minutes
Serves 10

1.5 kg thick sausages ▲ 6 onions, finely sliced ▲ 2 teaspoons
oil ▲ 60 g butter, melted ▲ 10 long bread rolls, buttered
▲ grated cheese ▲ shredded lettuce, sliced tomato, shredded
carrot, to serve ▲ coleslaw, to serve

1 Bring a large pan of water to the boil. Add sausages, reduce
heat and cook for 5 minutes. Drain and cool. Pierce sausages
with a fork or skewer.
2 Heat oil and butter in large frying pan; cook onion until
transparent. Move onions to one side of the pan; turn
occasionally to brown. Add sausages and cook 10–15 minutes
or until sausages have browned and onions are soft. (If
barbecuing, do this on a hotplate over hot part of the fire.)
3 Split rolls lengthways; serve with onions, sausages, cheese
and salad on a large platter. Serve coleslaw in a separate bowl.

ONION DIP

Preparation time: 15 minutes
Total cooking time: Nil *Serves* 6–8

45 g dried French onion soup ■ 2 tablespoons lemon juice
■ 3/4 cup softened cream cheese ■ 1 cup plain yoghurt
■ 1/4 cup chopped fresh parsley

1 Combine soup mix and lemon juice in large bowl; stand
30 minutes. Add cream cheese, yoghurt and parsley; mix
well. Refrigerate, covered, until needed.
2 Serve with crackers, bread sticks or vegetable sticks.

CHEESE **SWAGS**

Preparation time: 15 minutes *Total cooking time:* Nil
Makes 12

6 slices wholemeal bread ● 6 cheese sticks ● 6 slices luncheon
meat ● 12 chives

1 Remove crusts from bread and flatten with a rolling pin.
Place a slice of luncheon meat on each piece of bread, then a
cheese stick; roll up bread tightly.
2 Tie a chive fairly tightly around both ends of the roll,
approximately 3 cm in from the end. Cut rolls in half so that
the chive tie is in the centre of each Swag.

MAGGOT **MOUNDS**

Preparation time: 20 minutes *Total cooking time*: 12 minutes
Makes 60

**500 g desiccated coconut ♦ 410 g can condensed milk
♦ 2 teaspoons vanilla essence ♦ glacé cherries ♦ coloured
sprinkles and chocolate sprinkles, for decoration**

1 Preheat oven to moderate 180°C; grease two oven trays.
Combine coconut, condensed milk and vanilla in large bowl;
mix until thoroughly combined. Drop 2 teaspoonsful at a
time onto prepared trays, allowing room for spreading.
2 Decorate with glacé cherries and sprinkles. Bake 10–12
minutes or until lightly browned. Remove from trays
immediately and cool.

CHOC-CHERRY SPIDERS

Preparation time: 20 minutes *Total cooking time:* 5 minutes
Makes 20

**100 g glacé cherries, finely chopped ■ 1/3 cup flaked almonds,
toasted ■ 100 g fried egg noodles ■ 200 g dark chocolate,
chopped ■ 30 g butter ■ icing sugar, for dusting**

1 Line an oven tray with greaseproof paper. Combine
cherries, almonds and noodles in a bowl.
2 Place chocolate and butter in a small heatproof bowl; stand
bowl over pan of simmering water until chocolate has melted
and mixture is smooth. Remove from heat. Add chocolate to
cherry mixture. Stir gently to combine.
3 Drop heaped teaspoonfuls onto prepared tray. Leave to set.
Dust with icing sugar when firm.

HAM **AND** CHEESE **SCROLLS**

Preparation time: 10 minutes *Total cooking time:* 15 minutes
Makes 12

**340 g packet scone mix ● 2 tablespoons tomato sauce
● 1 cup grated cheddar cheese ● 1/2 cup finely chopped ham
● 1–2 tablespoons milk, to glaze**

1 Preheat oven to moderately hot 210°C (190°C gas). Make
up scone dough according to the directions on the packet.
Roll out scone dough to a 30 x 20 cm rectangle. Spread
with tomato sauce, sprinkle with cheese, then ham. Roll up
the dough.
2 Cut dough into 2 cm thick slices. Brush each with a little
milk. Place on a baking tray. Bake 15 minutes or until
golden. Serve warm.

CHOC-MINT **CONE** CAKES

Preparation time: 20 minutes *Total cooking time:* 20 minutes
Makes 24

**340 g packet chocolate cake mix ▲ 24 square-bottomed ice-
cream cones ▲ 24 after-dinner mints ▲ 24 Smarties**

1 Preheat oven to moderate 180°C; line two oven trays with
baking paper. Prepare cake mix according to the directions
on the packet.
2 Spoon 1 1/2 tablespoons of cake mixture into each cone.
Place cone on prepared trays. Bake 20 minutes or until the
cakes are firm when pressed with the back of a spoon.
Remove from oven and cool.
3 When cool, place an after-dinner mint on top of each cake.
Place cones in warm oven 1–2 minutes to melt mint slightly.
Place a Smartie on mint and serve.

TEDDY BEAR CAKES

Preparation time: 20 minutes *Total cooking time:* 15 minutes
Makes 12

340 g packet buttercake mix ■ 100 g dark chocolate dots
■ 1 cup chocolate hazelnut spread ■ 250 g honey-flavoured
mini teddy biscuits ■ 2 tablespoons hundreds and thousands

1 Preheat oven to moderate 180°C. Brush base and sides of a
12-cup muffin tin with oil. Prepare buttercake mix according
to directions on packet; fold chocolate dots through mixture.
2 Spoon mixture into prepared tins; bake 15 minutes or until
firm and golden brown. Allow to stand in tin 5 minutes.
Remove cakes and cool on wire rack.
3 Spread each with chocolate hazelnut spread. Place 4–5
teddy biscuits around the edge of cakes. Sprinkle hundreds
and thousands around biscuits.

STICKY BANANA BUNS

Preparation time: 20 minutes *Total cooking time:* 15 minutes
Makes 12

1/2 cup soft brown sugar ◆ 90 g butter ◆ 2 tablespoons
sultanas ◆ 2 1/2 cups plain flour ◆ 2 teaspoons baking powder
◆ 2 ripe bananas, mashed ◆ 1/2 cup milk ◆ 30 g butter, extra,
melted ◆ 2 tablespoons soft brown sugar, extra

1 Preheat oven to moderate 180°C. Combine sugar and 30 g
butter in a small pan. Stir over a medium heat until sugar has
melted. Stir in sultanas. Spoon mixture into a 12-cup muffin
tin. Sift flour and baking powder into bowl. Add remaining
butter and rub into flour until it resembles coarse
breadcrumbs. Make a well in the centre; add bananas and
milk. Mix with a flat-bladed knife until a soft dough forms.
2 Knead dough lightly on a floured surface until smooth.
Roll out to a rectangle 20 x 15 cm. Brush with extra melted
butter and sprinkle with extra sugar. Roll up lengthwise
firmly and cut into 12 equal slices. Place in muffin tin, cut-
side down. Bake 15 minutes. Cool on a wire rack.

WHITE CHRISTMAS

Preparation time: 20 minutes + 1 hour refrigeration
Total cooking time: 5 minutes *Makes* 24

100 g coloured glacé cherries, halved ● 100 g chopped glacé
pineapple ● 1/2 cup mixed dried fruit ● 3 cups Rice Bubbles
● 1 cup desiccated coconut ● 1 cup full-cream milk powder
● 2/3 cup icing sugar, sifted ● 250 g white vegetable
shortening (copha), melted

1 Line a 30 x 20 cm baking tray with foil. Combine cherries,
pineapple, fruit, Rice Bubbles, coconut, milk powder and
icing sugar in a bowl; make a well in the centre; add
shortening and mix well. Press mixture into tray. Flatten with
a spoon. Refrigerate one hour. Cut into fingers when firm.

*Left to right: Maggot Mounds, Choc-cherry Spiders,
Ham and Cheese Scrolls, Choc-mint Cone Cakes,
Teddy Bear Cakes, Sticky Banana Buns, White Christmas*

Left to right: Stained Glass Biscuits, Choc-chip Fudge, Pizza, American Hot Dogs, Hot Bean Dogs and Hot Dog Boats, Ham and Egg Rolls, Choc-coated Iceblocks, Toffee Muesli Bars

STAINED GLASS BISCUITS

Preparation time: 40 minutes *Total cooking time:* 10 minutes per batch *Makes* 35

125 g butter ▲ ¹/₃ cup caster sugar ▲ ¹/₄ cup golden syrup ▲ 1 egg ▲ 2¹/₂ cups plain flour ▲ 200 g boiled sweets, crushed ▲ 1 egg yolk, lightly beaten

1 Preheat oven to moderately hot 210°C (190°C gas). Line 2 oven trays with baking paper. Using electric beaters, beat butter, sugar and syrup until light and creamy. Add egg; beat well. Sift flour into mixture; mix with a knife until well combined. Turn dough onto lightly floured surface and knead gently 1 minute. Roll out to 5 mm thickness.
2 Using large biscuit cutters, cut shapes from dough. Place on prepared trays. Cut contrasting shapes in centre of biscuits; remove centres. Brush biscuits with egg yolk. Bake 5 minutes.
3 Spoon sweets into middle of biscuits, piling them fairly high. Bake another 5 minutes or until sweets melt: cool.

CHOC-CHIP FUDGE

Preparation time: 10 minutes + overnight refrigeration *Total cooking time:* 15 minutes *Makes* 24

400 g can sweetened condensed milk ■ 90 g butter ■ 2 tablespoons cocoa powder, sifted ■ ²/₃ cup slivered almonds ■ 1 teaspoon vanilla essence ■ 1 cup dark choc bits

1 Line a 26 x 8 x 4 cm bar tin with foil. Heat condensed milk and butter in small pan over low heat. Add cocoa and mix well. Stir gently with wooden spoon 10 minutes.
2 Remove from heat; add almonds and vanilla. Whisk 2 minutes; add choc bits. Whisk again until thick and smooth. Spread into tin. Refrigerate overnight; cut into squares.

PIZZA

Preparation time: 20 minutes *Total cooking time:* 25–30 minutes *Serves* 8

¹/₂ teaspoon sugar ▲ ¹/₂ teaspoon salt ▲ 7 g dried yeast ▲ 1 cup warm water ▲ 2 tablespoons vegetable oil ▲ 2³/₄ cups plain flour ▲ ¹/₄ cup tomato paste ▲ 2 cups grated cheese ▲ 1 cup pineapple pieces, well drained ▲ ¹/₂ cup chopped ham ▲ ¹/₄ cup chopped salami ▲ 2 cabanossi, sliced ▲ 1 capsicum, diced ▲ 4 mushrooms, sliced

1 Preheat oven to moderately hot 210°C (190°C gas). Brush a 30 cm round pizza tray with melted butter or oil. Combine sugar, salt, yeast and warm water in a small bowl. Cover bowl with plastic wrap and stand 10 minutes in a warm place.
2 Sift flour into large bowl. Make a well in the centre; add the yeast mixture and mix well. Knead the dough on a lightly floured surface 5 minutes or until smooth and elastic. Roll out on a lightly floured surface to form a 35 cm circle. (Dough should be larger than pizza tray.)
3 Transfer to tray; tuck in extra dough to form a rim. Spread evenly with tomato paste; sprinkle with half the grated cheese, then sprinkle with pineapple, ham, salami, cabanossi, capsicum and mushrooms. Top with remaining cheese and bake 25–30 minutes or until crust is crisp.

AMERICAN **HOT** DOGS

Preparation time: 20 minutes
Total cooking time: 10 minutes *Serves* 10

**10 frankfurts ■ 10 long hot dog rolls ■ American-style
mustard and tomato sauce, for topping**

1 Cook frankfurts in pan of simmering water 5–10 minutes.
Split rolls lengthways. Remove frankfurts from water. Place
in roll. Top with mustard and sauce.
HOT BEAN DOGS: Make as above, omitting mustard;
top with warmed baked beans and grated cheddar cheese.
HOT DOG BOATS: Make as above, omitting mustard.
Cut 5 cheddar cheese slices in half diagonally. Thread half a
wooden skewer through 2 corners. Skewer into hot dog.

HAM AND EGG **ROLL**

Preparation time: 10 minutes *Total cooking time:* 8 minutes
Makes 8

**4 English muffins ▲ 1 cup grated cheese ▲ 50 g butter
▲ 4 eggs, lightly beaten ▲ 2 tablespoons chopped parsley
▲ ground pepper ▲ 1/2 cup chopped ham**

1 Cut muffins in half; remove a little of the bread to make a
cavity. Fill cavity with grated cheese. Melt butter in small
pan. Add eggs and cook over low heat, stirring constantly,
until light and thick. Spoon into muffin; sprinkle eggs with
parsley, pepper and ham. Place under grill 2–3 minutes or
until hot and muffin is lightly toasted.

CHOC-COATED **ICEBLOCKS**

Preparation time: 5 minutes + 6 hours freezing
Total cooking time: Nil *Makes* 10

**pulp of 2 small passionfruit ■ 450 g can crushed pineapple
■ 1/4 cup plain yoghurt ■ 10 icy-pole sticks ■ chocolate ice-
ice-cream topping, for drizzling**

1 Combine passionfruit pulp and drained pineapple in small
bowl; stir in yoghurt. Spoon mixture into iceblock moulds or
waxed-paper cups. Place an icy-pole stick in each iceblock.
Place iceblocks in freezer about 6 hours or until frozen.
2 Remove iceblocks from moulds and drizzle with chocolate
topping just before serving.

TOFFEE MUESLI **BARS**

Preparation time: 10 minutes *Total cooking time:* 25 minutes
Makes 24

**1 cup sugar ♦ 2 tablespoons honey ♦ 2 tablespoons glucose
syrup ♦ 50 g butter ♦ 1/3 cup water ♦ 400 g untoasted muesli**

1 Line base and sides of a shallow 28 x 18 cm cake tin with
foil. Brush foil with melted butter or oil.
2 Combine sugar, honey, glucose, butter and water in a
medium heavy-based pan. Stir over medium heat, without
boiling, until sugar has completely dissolved. Brush sugar
crystals from sides of pan with a wet pastry brush. Bring to
the boil, reduce heat slightly, boil without stirring for
20 minutes. Remove pan from heat immediately.
3 Place muesli in a warmed bowl. Pour in toffee and stir to
combine. Pour into tin; smooth surface. Score into 24 bars
while still warm. Allow to set. When cool, cut into bars.

PARTY DRINKS

FOAMING CRATERS

In a blender or food processor, process 250 g washed and hulled strawberries until smooth. Divide puree evenly between eight tall tumblers. Place a scoop of vanilla ice-cream in each glass and top with lemonade, being careful not to overfill glass. Serve immediately.
Serves 8

MOO JUICE

Combine 400 g fruit-flavoured yoghurt, 2 tablespoons honey, 1 teaspoon vanilla essence, 2 ripe peeled bananas, 2 cups chilled milk and 4 scoops vanilla ice-cream in a blender. Cover and blend at high speed for 3 minutes. Divide between eight glasses and sprinkle with a little grated nutmeg. Serve immediately.
Serves 8

POISON POTION

Pour 1 tablespoon each of lime and raspberry cordials into a large glass. Top with lemonade. Place a scoop of chocolate ice-cream on top. Allow to stand 1 minute before serving.
Serves 1

JUNGLE JUICE

In a large serving bowl, combine 850 ml unsweetened pineapple juice, 3 cups apple juice and 450 g can unsweetened crushed pineapple. Stir lightly to combine; cover and refrigerate at least 1 hour. Just before serving, add 750 ml chilled lemonade or dry ginger ale. Garnish with mint and glacé cherries.
Serves 8
NOTE: Substitute orange and mango juice for apple juice, if preferred.

Having fun is thirsty work,
so have plenty of cool refreshments standing by

FRUIT PUNCH

In a large serving bowl, combine 125 ml can orange juice, 425 g can fruit salad, the juice of 1 orange and the juice of 1 lemon. Stir lightly to combine; cover and refrigerate at least 1 hour. Just before serving add 750 ml chilled lemonade. Garnish with fresh fruit such as raspberries, blueberries, apple, orange, rockmelon and honeydew melon.
Serves 10

PINEAPPLE CREAM CRUSH

Combine 450 g can undrained crushed pineapple and 1 cup pineapple juice in a large jug. Slowly add 200 ml coconut milk, whisking continually until well blended. To serve, pour into tall glasses over plenty of ice. Garnish with pineapple slices. Serve immediately.
Serves 2

CACTUS JUICE

Peel and seed $1/2$ a cucumber and slice finely. Place in a large serving jug or bowl with 2 litres apple juice and 2 tablespoons honey. Stir lightly to combine; cover and refrigerate at least 1 hour. Just before serving, add 750 ml chilled lemonade and 750 ml soda water. Top with ice-cubes. Garnish with mint leaves.
Serves 8
COOL BREEZE: Make as above, leaving out cucumber.

WITCHES' BREW

Pour 100 ml cola into a large glass. Add a scoop of vanilla ice-cream. Stir gently to foam (mixture will 'boil over' if stirred too hard). Drizzle $1/2$ teaspoon strawberry syrup over the top. Hang 1 or 2 lolly snakes over the edge of the glass.
Serves 1
MOTOR OIL: Make as above, leaving out snakes.
COLA SPIDER: Leave out syrup and snakes.

Left to right: Fruit Punch, Pineapple Cream Crush, Cactus Juice, Witches' Brew, Foaming Crater, Moo Juice, Poison Potion, Jungle Juice

PEACH DREAM

Combine 425 g can drained peach slices, 500 ml vanilla ice-cream, 1/4 cup orange juice, 2–3 drops vanilla essence and 2 cups chilled milk in a blender; blend until smooth. Serve at once in tumblers, garnished with orange slices.
Serves 4

ANT CORDIAL

Combine 3 cups water and 3 cups sugar in large pan; stir over medium heat until sugar dissolves. Bring to the boil, then reduce heat; simmer 10 minutes. Remove from heat to cool. Add pulp of 12 large passionfruit; cover and refrigerate at least 1 hour. Just before serving, pour 2 tablespoons passionfruit syrup into a large tumbler. Top with iced water or chilled soda water. Garnish with kiwi fruit slices.
Serves 10

RUDOLPH'S PUNCH

Combine 3 cups water and 3 cups sugar in large pan; stir over medium heat until sugar dissolves. Bring to the boil, then reduce heat; simmer 10 minutes. Remove from heat to cool. When cool combine in a large punch bowl with 850 ml pineapple juice, 1 cup orange juice, juice of 2 large lemons, pulp of 2 passionfruit, 5 cups cold black tea and 500 ml dry ginger ale; add ice. Garnish with fresh fruit and mint sprigs.
Serves 10

CHOCOLATE FLOAT

In a jug, combine 4 cups cold milk and 1/4 cup chocolate syrup or topping; stir well to combine. Cover and refrigerate at least 1 hour. Just before serving, whisk mixture until foamy. Place a scoop of vanilla ice-cream in each serving glass and top with chocolate mixture. Serve immediately.
Serves 4

Left to right: Peach Dream, Ant Cordial, Rudolph's Punch, Chocolate Float, Malted Milkshake, Banana Yoghurt Smoothie, Lemon Thirst, Mango Wizz

MALTED MILKSHAKE

Combine 1 cup milk, 1 tablespoon powdered drinking chocolate, 1 tablespoon powdered malt and 4 scoops vanilla ice-cream in blender. Blend on high 1 minute or until all ingredients are combined. Pour into glasses and serve immediately.
Serves 2

BANANA YOGHURT SMOOTHIE

Combine 1 cup cold milk, 1 peeled and sliced banana, 1 tablespoon honey, 1 egg, 2 tablespoons yoghurt, 2 scoops vanilla ice-cream and 2 ice cubes in a blender. Blend on high 2 minutes or until smooth. Pour into glasses to serve. Sprinkle with wheat-germ and garnish with a slice of banana.
Serves 2

LEMON THIRST

Peel rind from 4 lemons; place in a pan with $1^1/_2$ cups sugar and 2 cups water. Simmer gently 20 minutes. Strain and set aside until cold. Stir 1 cup lemon juice and 1 litre extra water into the cold syrup and chill well. Serve in tall tumblers over crushed ice and top each with a lemon slice. Serves 8

MANGO WIZZ

Place 20 ice cubes in blender or food processor. Process until ice is roughly chopped. Add 3 cups fresh mango pieces. Process until fruit and ice are well combined. Pour mixture into tall glasses and serve immediately. Garnish with mango slice and pineapple leaf. Serves 2

Take-Home TReaTS

FAIRIes

■ **SPIRIT** the fairies home with a little extra magic. This selection of treats includes pretty pink lollies, jelly hearts, Fairy Wand biscuits (recipe page 42) and a bag of sparkling Star Dust (recipe page 49).

OUTeR SPACe

■ **TIME** to blast off, so send them home with this simple hand-decorated paper plate, a selection of disc-shaped sweets and some energy food for the long journey back to Earth.

A parcel of goodies to take home is a fitting way to end the party

DINOSAURS

■ **THE** birthday child can help make these simple take-home bags: cut out a ragged edge on a brown paper bag and attach dinosaur stickers. Fill with jelly dinosaurs, bubble gum and anything that looks 'prehistoric'.

PIRATES

■ **A TREASURE** trove to remember the party by. The packaging can be elaborate, as pictured here, or a simple bag. Include some chocolate pieces of eight and some gaudy 'jewels' in the form of coloured jellies.

BEACH

■ **A KISS** of sunshine in every box, even when the sun's gone down. Pack the box with crystallised pawpaw, banana chips, jelly pineapples and fun fish-shaped sweets and lollipops.

SNOW

■ **TOTALLY COOL.** Twist a large paper doily into a cone shape and fill it full of things that suggest winter—cool white mints, frosted sweets and coconut ice.

ZOO

■ **MUFFLE** tummy growls with a feed bag made from hessian (if you're keen) or brown paper (if you're not). Fill it with good things like Animal Feed (recipe page 51) and herds of jelly animals.

ROBOTS & COMPUTERS

■ **CHIPS** are the theme of this take-home package—potato chips, choc-chip biscuits, anything small and round. Pile them into plastic goblets and wrap in techno-blue cellophane.

ARABIAN NIGHTS

■ **OPEN** sesame. Aladdin's selection of exotic delights contains Desert Sand (recipe on page 49) Turkish Delight, pastel sweets and 'Magic Carpet' biscuits.

HALLOWEEN

■ **TAKE** this home and put it under the pillow, if you dare. Black cats, slimy worms and jelly snakes and spiders all squirm together in this simple hand–decorated paper bag.

THE GREAT OUTDOORS

■ LITTLE ones can take a touch of the outdoors indoors with this bag full of wriggling, writhing wildlife. The bag, which has been hand-decorated with a trail of ants, contains chocolate beetles, jelly snakes and flies and insect lollipops.

HIPPIES

■ MAKE brown the theme of this earthy assortment. Choose caramels, nut and seed bars and chocolate-coated licorice. (The kids will enjoy making the bags.)

TeDDY Bears PiCnic

■ **BEARS,** bears everywhere. Choose from the many bear-shaped biscuits and sweets available, display them in a 'picnic' basket and wrap prettily with cellophane.

CHrISTmas

■ **THIS** traditional selection of treats features Stained Glass Biscuits and White Christmas (see page 63) as well as humbugs and licorice allsorts. The felt bag can hang from the Christmas tree.

WILD WEST

■ **AS THE** sun sinks slowly in the West, it's time to round up the youngsters and shoo them home. This selection includes chocolate bullets, star pretzels, Wagon Wheel biscuits and licorice 'lariats'.

PUNK

■ **HEADBANGERS** and grunge grommets will appreciate this 'filthy' collection of treats——War Heads, gobstoppers and tingling sweets—anything that finishes the party with a bang!

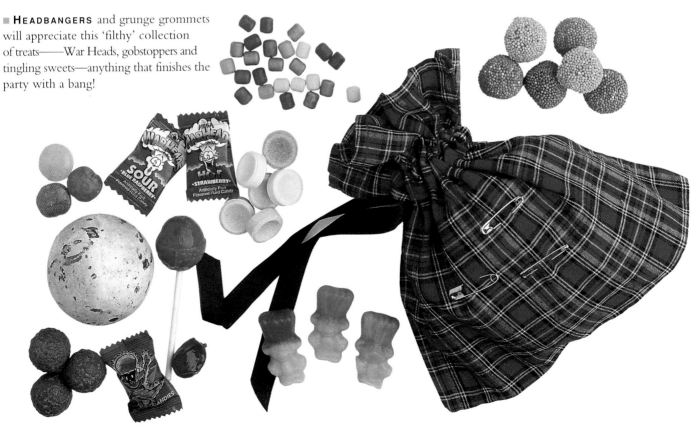

SPORT

■ **THE** full-time whistle blows and a surge of energy is needed. Decorate a wax drinking cup with sporty stickers and fill it with plenty of sweet things.

CIRCUS

■ **BURSTING** with colour, this take-home bag, puchased from the supermarket, is a vivid reminder of all the fun of the Big Top. (Make sure you include some coloured popcorn.)

DISCO

■ **BOOGIE** Wonderland comes to life with this cornucopia of glitzy treats. Shape shiny wrapping paper into a cone and fill with jelly red lips and spangly sweets.

UNDERWATER

■ **WHEN** it's time to resurface, kids can remember the party with Popcorn Pearls (recipe page 53) jelly sea creatures and Lifesavers packed in a cup decorated simply, but effectively, with stickers.

Party GAMES

Balloon Games

BALLOON FIGHT

GIVE EVERY CHILD a balloon labelled with her name. Children throw their balloon into the air and try to keep it up there, while at the same time trying to knock other balloons to the ground. The winner is the last player with a balloon in the air.

BALLOON HOP

DIVIDE CHILDREN INTO teams and have them line up behind their leader. Assign each team a colour and place a pile of balloons in that colour at the opposite end of the room. There should be one balloon for each player. At the signal, the leader hops across the room, picks up a balloon of the team's colour and hops back with it to the team. When he returns, the next player hops across to find a balloon, and so on until each player has a balloon. When the last player returns with his balloon, all the players on the team blow up their balloons and tie the necks. (If a player has trouble tying a balloon, another player in the team may help.) The first team with all its balloons blown up and tied wins.

BALLOON VOLLEYBALL

SUSPEND A PIECE of string across the room or play area, at approximately head height. Divide players into two teams and position them on either side of the string. One team serves by hitting the balloon over the string and the other team must return the balloon without allowing it to fall to the ground. When the balloon cannot be returned, the other team scores a point. The first team to score twenty is the winner. This is a good indoor game for boisterous youngsters forced inside by rain. Make sure you clear furniture and breakables well away from play.

BAT THE BALLOON

DIVIDE THE CHILDREN into two teams and seat them cross-legged on the floor facing each other. While staying seated the children toss a balloon to the opposing team, trying to tap it over the children's heads and onto the ground behind their backs. Teams gain a point every time they bat the balloon out of the other team's reach.

All children love party games.
Here are new suggestions, as well as the old favourites

BROOMSTICK RELAY

MARK TWO PARALLEL lines approximately 3 metres apart, and call one the starting line. Divide the children into pairs, then line them up facing each other behind the lines. Each child at the starting line has a broom and a balloon. The child must sweep the balloon towards their opposite number, who must then sweep it back again. Bursting balloons disqualify sweepers, and the first pair to successfully complete the relay wins.

HOP AND POP

TIE A BALLOON to the ankle of each player. Children have to burst other's balloons by any means—stomping or pinching—while keeping their own intact. A player is disqualified once his or her balloon bursts.

WHIZZING BALLOONS

CHILDREN STAND behind a line; each has a balloon of a different colour or marked with the child's name. The child blows up the balloon and holds it by the neck until the signal. Children let go of their balloon—the balloon that travels furthest from the release point wins. This is a simple game, requiring no skill which will appeal to younger children. Some children may need assistance blowing up balloons.

WILD WEST WIND

ESTABLISH A starting and finishing line about 3 metres apart. Position the children along the starting line and give each a round balloon and a straw. The children have to race on their hands and knees, blowing their balloon with the straw. The first child to reach the finishing line wins.
Note: This game can also be played as a relay.

HUNTiNG & HiDiNG

SCAVENGER HUNT

GIVE EACH player (or pair of players) a list of objects to find and collect within a determined length of time. For children who read well, write the list on a paper bag, which can then be used for collecting the items. The list can be made simple for the very young children who have just begun to read (alternatively, assign an older helper to each child), or quite complicated for older children. You can decide whether to include theme-related objects that you have 'planted' around the party area, or only objects that are lying about your house and garden in good quantities. The first to collect all items on the list is the winner. A simple list might include a piece of string, a flower, a gum leaf, a round stone, a feather and so on.

MAGPIES

THIS IS A miniature 'Scavenger Hunt' that can be played throughout the duration of the party. At the very start of the party, each child is given an empty matchbox with his or her name on it. The object of the game is for each player to collect as many tiny things as can be fitted into the matchbox. Grains of sand or sugar are not counted. At the end of the party the matchboxes are collected and the contents counted. The player who has collected the highest number of objects is the winner.

PARTNERS

BEFORE THE PARTY, draw up a list of famous storybook partners—Little Red Riding Hood and the Wolf, Alice in Wonderland and the White Rabbit, Cinderella and the Prince and so on. Write each name on a piece of paper. At the start of the game, pin a name on the back of each child, not allowing them to see their own names. Each child must establish who he or she is, by asking questions of the other players. ('Am I an animal? What colour am I?') Answers should be given in the form of clues— 'You're green'—without giving away the name, until players arrive at the right identity. Once all the children have correctly guessed who they are, they search for their partners, whose names, of course, they can see. This is a good way to pair children up for other games such as a Back-to-Back Race or Hat Making.

POSTMAN'S HOLIDAY

YOU WILL NEED ten boxes, each with a posting slot and labelled with a different town or street name related to the party's theme. The boxes are hidden around the house or garden. Each player gets ten envelopes, addressed to each box. Starting from a common central point, players pick up one envelope at a time, write their initials on the back, then run off to post it in the right box. They then run back for another envelope. They must post their ten envelopes as fast as possible. When they have all done so, open the boxes and check the envelopes inside. The player with the most posted correctly wins. *Variation:* Postman's Island Holiday (for the Beach party) is played exactly as above, except that the boxes are labelled with the names of South Sea islands.

PRESENT HUNT

AS EACH PLAYER arrives, she is given a piece of paper with a written clue to guide her to her present. To avoid mistakes, make sure the presents are labelled with the children's names.

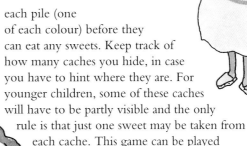

THE **RING** GAME

ARRANGE THE children in a circle with one in the middle. The children hold a circle of string, onto which is threaded a ring. The centre child closes his eyes tightly and counts silently up to twenty. While he is doing this, the children in the circle slide the ring from hand to hand around the string, concealing it under their hands. When the child in the middle has reached twenty, he opens his eyes and tries to spot which player is holding the ring. If he guesses correctly, the player holding the ring changes places with him. If not, the child stays in the centre.

SARDINES

ALL CHILDREN EXCEPT one count to twenty together while the odd one out goes into hiding. When they reach twenty the children must hunt for the missing child. Whoever finds the child has to join him in hiding. Eventually all but one child will be squashed into the one hiding place. When the last child discovers the hiding place, the game can be played again with the child who found the hiding place first taking a turn as the next hider.

STRING **HUNT**

ALLOW A BALL of string for each guest; tie one end of the string to a small present and place the present where it can be seen. Unwind the ball of string, making a trail across chairs, under tables, around door knobs, under rugs and so on, making it tricky and moderately tangled, depending on the age group. As the guests arrive, each is given her ball of string and starts to wind up the string, following it until she reaches the present. (It is a good idea to put breakables out of the way while the game is in progress.)

TREASURE HUNT

BEFORE THE PARTY, hide caches of foil-wrapped sweets, a different colour for each pile, in secret places around your house and garden. When the children arrive tell them how many piles of sweets there are. They must collect a sweet from each pile (one of each colour) before they can eat any sweets. Keep track of how many caches you hide, in case you have to hint where they are. For younger children, some of these caches will have to be partly visible and the only rule is that just one sweet may be taken from each cache. This game can be played throughout the duration of the party, in conjunction with another game such as Hide and Seek, or as an entity on its own with a time limit.

CAP**TIVES**

DIVIDE CHILDREN into two teams, the Sheriffs and the Bandits. Sheriffs cover their eyes and count to 100 while the Bandits scatter throughout the house and hide. The Sheriffs then seek out all those in hiding. When a Sheriff finds a Bandit, he or she is taken captive and put in a 'jailhouse' nominated at the beginning of the game. The first captured Bandit must hold onto the jailhouse bars—the leg of a table or the side of a chair—with one hand. The next captive must hold hands with the first. Each succeeding captive holds hands with the last, so that the captives form a chain.

Meanwhile, those Bandits who are still in hiding have to sneak back to the jailhouse and free the captives as quietly as possible. A Bandit may free only one captive at a time, and must free the captive who is last in the chain. A captive is freed by a touch on the shoulder. Once free, Bandits go off to hide again. The object of the game is for the Sheriffs to capture all the Bandits—this may take a while.

BLINDFOLD DRAWING

GIVE EACH blindfolded player a piece of paper and a pencil, and a subject to draw that is related to the party's theme. When the players think they have completed their drawing, ask for some additions to be made, for example, 'Put a pom-pom on the clown's hat', or 'Draw a flower in his buttonhole'. The winning picture is the one voted the funniest or the best by the other players. This game can also be played non-competitively and is a good one for calm-down times.

PIN THE TAIL ON THE DONKEY

DRAW AN OUTLINE of a tailless donkey on a large sheet of paper. Mark a large cross where the tail should be attached. Hang up the picture at the children's eye level and give the first child a paper or rope donkey's tail with a drawing pin in one end. Blindfold the child, spin him around three times and point him in the general direction of the donkey. Mark the spot the child has chosen to place the tail with the child's initials and go on to the next child. The one who puts the tail on, or nearest to, the correct spot wins.

VARIATIONS: Pin the Tail on the Triceratops, Pin the Tail on the Camel and Pin the Tail on the Rat are all played as above, except that, of course, the drawing differs. You can do these yourself, either free-hand if you feel confident or by choosing a simple illustration from a book, enlarging it on a photocopier and tracing it onto paper.

BLINDFOLD Games

THESE GAMES ARE BEST FOR CHILDREN FOUR AND OVER

ANIMALIA

BLINDFOLD six children. Let the others watch. Line up the blindfolded children in a row, not using their names, so that they do not know who their neighbours are. Taking each in turn, and identifying her by touch only, give her the name of an animal: snake, lion and so on. Let each child practise the sound of her animal, hissing, grunting, roaring and so on. Then get them to move out of line and turn around a few times, until the line is thoroughly muddled. The blindfolded children then have to remake the row in its original order, by listening to the sounds made by each other and placing themselves in the right relative position. Remaining children watch to see if the order is correctly achieved. Observers and players then swap places.

GUESS WHAT

PREPARE A NUMBER of saucers containing different distinctive foods, such as tomato sauce, curry powder, chocolate, pepper or lemons. Blindfold all the children and lead them to the table one by one. Ask them to identify the foods by smell or feel. The children who have had their turn can watch the others, but, of course, cannot call out the answers.

This game can also involve identifying food by taste. Make sure the food is edible but potentially 'disgusting', such as tinned spaghetti, whipped cream or jelly rats.

BLINDMAN'S BUFF

BLINDFOLD ONE child and spin her around three times. The other players must move around making noise and so on while the blindfolded player tries to catch them. When she catches a child, she must guess who it is. If she guesses correctly, the caught child takes over as the blind man.

SQUEAK, PIGGY, SQUEAK!

CHILDREN SIT ON chairs around the room. Blindfold one child, turn him around a few times and give him a cushion. While the children sit as silently as possible, the 'blind' player must find a child, sit on his lap with the cushion and call out 'Squeak, piggy, squeak!' The child makes a piggy noise. If the blind player correctly guesses whose lap he is sitting on, he changes places with him. Children should rearrange themselves and their chairs before starting again.

THIEVES

BLINDFOLD ONE child and give her a rolled newspaper to hold. Sit the blindfolded child in the middle of a circle made by other children. In the middle of the circle is a pile of treasure—necklaces, brooches, bracelets, and so on. The children take it in turns trying to steal an item of treasure. If the blindfolded child hears a thief, she strikes at him with the newspaper and calls 'Thief! Thief!' If she touches the thief, he must return empty-handed to his place to wait for his next turn. The thief who collects the most treasure wins the game.

PRIZE SUGGESTIONS

THERE are many prizes that will do duty for any party, no matter what its theme, or whether it has a theme at all. All children love water pistols, for example, and will not be able to resist playing with them straight away. Do bear this in mind if you are giving them out as prizes and your party is confined indoors or the guests are wearing their best party clothes.

GIANT novelty sunglasses can be bought, often in packs of two or three, from disposal shops. Skipping ropes are also inexpensive prizes which can be used in a race.

MUSICAL GAMES

GODS AND GODDESSES

THIS GAME requires fairly slow and gentle music. Give each child a book. When the music starts, the children walk around the room balancing the books on their heads. When the music stops, the children must try to go down on one knee. If their book falls off, he or she is eliminated. The music starts again and the game continues. The last child left in the game is the winner.

HIGH STEPPERS

MAKE HURDLES by placing two chairs together with their seats facing each other. Place these around the play area to form a wide circle. Ask the children to form themselves into pairs. When the music begins, the children march around the circle, climbing over the hurdles as they come to them. When the music stops, any pair touching a hurdle is eliminated. The winning pair is the last one left in the game.

HOT POTATO

THE CHILDREN SIT in a circle. They pass around a ball as the music plays. When the music stops the child holding the ball is eliminated from the circle. The last child to be eliminated is the winner.

JUMP THE BROOM

PUT A BROOM on the ground. Play music as the children skip round in a circle, jumping over the broom. When the music stops, the child jumping over the broom, or the last child to jump the broom, is out. Continue until there is one child left.

LIMBO

PLAY THIS GAME to a lively background of West Indian music. Two people, preferably adults, hold either end of a 2-metre length of dowelling at chest height. They should hold the stick in cupped hands, so that it will fall easily if touched. The children take turns going under the stick, bending their knees and leaning as far back as necessary. No hands may touch the floor. This will be easy at first, but with each round the stick gets lower. Anyone who falls or touches the ground with their hands is eliminated.

MUSICAL CHAIRS

MAKE TWO LINES of back-to-back chairs. There should be one less chair than the number of children. When the music starts, children march around the chairs. When the music stops everyone sits down. The person without a chair drops out. Remove a chair and start the music again. The game continues until only two players are left competing for the last chair.

MUSICAL BLACKOUT

THIS IS PLAYED like Musical Chairs except that when the music stops, the lights are also switched off for five seconds. When the lights are switched on again, any player who has not found a chair is eliminated.

MUSICAL BUMPS

THE CHILDREN dance about as music plays. When it stops, all players must immediately sit down. The last one to sit is out. The game goes on until only the winner is left.

MUSICAL **STATUES**

PLAY AS FOR Musical Bumps except that when the music stops, the children have to 'freeze' in position and remain as still as statues. Anyone who twitches is out.

MUSICAL HATS

THIS IS PLAYED using a hat for all but one player. Everyone stands or sits in a circle, facing the same direction. When the music starts, each player takes the hat from the head of the person in front and puts it on. When the music stops, the person without a hat is eliminated. Remove one hat from the game and continue until only one person (and one hat) is left.

MUSICAL **HOTCH** POTCH

PLACE A PILE of soft toys, numbering one fewer than the number of children, in the centre of the room. When the music starts, children hop or dance around the pile. When the music stops, the children must dive for an article from the pile. The child left without a toy is eliminated. Remove one of the toys and continue until only the winner remains. *Note:* This game could result in bumped heads, so choose relatively large toys.

MUSICAL ISLANDS

SCATTER SMALL MATS, newspapers, pieces of cardboard or suchlike over the floor to form 'islands'. When the music starts, children walk around in a circle. When the music stops, children must find an island to stand on. More than one child may stand on an island. Anyone unable to cram onto an island or who falls off into the 'water' is eliminated. The music starts again and the game continues. Remove islands during the game so that eventually many children are all trying to stand on a small spot. The last player left in the game is the winner.

MUSICAL **MAGIC** CARPET

CHOOSE A PART of the floor as a 'magic patch', but keep its position a secret. When the music starts, the children dance around in pairs. When the music stops, the children freeze. The pair nearest the magic patch wins a prize, and the game continues until all the prizes have been awarded. Alternatively, the game can be played for points. The pair nearest the magic patch scores a point, and the game is won by the pair with the most points after an agreed time.

GRAND CHAIN

DIVIDE PLAYERS into pairs and place them around the room. Give each player a balloon which has to be held between the knees. When the music begins, the pairs must join hands and walk around the room in time to the music. Any pair losing a balloon is eliminated. The last pair left parading with balloons wedged between their knees wins the game.

PRIZE **SUGGESTIONS**

THE little fairies will enjoy receiving a handmade wand for their efforts. (These can be made beforehand from glitter, cardboard, a drinking straw, ribbon and a little help from the birthday girl.)

FOR outdoor types and budding entomologists, a plastic 'bug-catcher', a magnifying glass, an ant farm, or a butterfly net is an appropriate reward.

MUSICAL SETS

THE CHILDREN SKIP about the room as the music plays. When the music stops, call out a number. The children must scramble to form a number set. Call out a number that must leave one child out; for example, call 'four' for seventeen children and four sets will form with one child remaining. That player drops out. Continue the game until there is only one player left.

MUSICAL TORCH

WHEN THE CHILDREN are sitting in a circle, the lights are turned out. When the music plays, children pass a torch around the circle, at just under chin level so that the face of each child is lit up. Whoever is left holding the torch when the music stops has to drop out. A stout plastic torch is best for this game, as it will probably be dropped. Play 'scary' music for this game and the eerie effect on the face when a torch is held under it will be amplified.

PASS THE PARCEL

PREPARE THE PARCEL beforehand. Wrap a prize in many layers of newspaper. For very young children place a sweet between each layer, or scatter smaller prizes randomly throughout the sheets of newspaper. The children sit round in a circle and pass the parcel to each other as the music plays. When the music stops, the child holding the parcel can unwrap a layer. The music starts again and the passing continues. Eventually the music stops for the last layer of wrapping, leaving the winner holding the prize.

MYSTERY PARCEL

PREPARE A PARCEL as for Pass the Parcel, but with a message written on each layer. Typical messages are 'Give to the girl with the darkest eyes!' or 'Pass to the person on your left!' The parcel is passed around to music. When the music stops, the child holding the parcel reads out the message and hands the parcel to the child who fits the description in the message. This child then unwraps the next layer of paper and the music restarts.

REFLEXES

FOR THIS FAST-PACED game, you will need a portable cassette player. Invite one of the players to operate the music (although perhaps the host should demonstrate what to do by playing the first round). The music operator stands with his back to the other players but must be clearly seen. The other players sit facing the operator's back. The operator switches on the music, and the other players have to guess when the operator is going to turn off the music. The players must stand up when they think the music is being turned off. (Of course, there will be some players who stand up too soon, and others who remain seated when the music cuts out.) The operator should make exaggerated or false movements that will fool the other players. The last one to rise when the music stops gets a point. Any players left sitting lose a point. The first player to five points is the winner, and becomes the music operator for the next round.

memory games

MEMORY TEST

MAKE A SELECTION of about twenty common objects such as a spoon, key, button, book, sweet, pen, paperclip, safety pin and so on. Place them on a tray and cover them with a cloth. Give each child a pencil and paper. The children gather round and the cloth is removed for two minutes. Cover the tray and take it away. The children have to write down as many objects as they can remember. The child who makes the longest correct list within a set time limit is the winner.

I WENT TO MARS

THE CHILDREN SIT in a circle. The first child announces 'I went to Mars and I took a . . .' then names any object. For example, the child might say: 'I went to Mars and I took a pencil.' The next child has to repeat this and add another object to the list. For example: 'I went to Mars and I took a pencil and an apple.' The third will add a new object, always keeping the list in order: 'I went to Mars and I took a pencil, an apple and my dog.' The game continues around the circle for as long as possible.
Variation: I Asked the Genie of the Lamp can be played at the Arabian Nights party. Simply substitute the words. This game can be adapted easily to most party themes.

MISMATCHES

DIVIDE THE CHILDREN into two teams. One team leaves the room while the other makes 'mismatches' by altering things in the room. They might change the position of an object, such as turning a vase upside down, or might change something about a person, such as putting a coat on inside out. At the end of a time limit the other team returns and tries to spot the mismatches. Any mismatches that have not been noticed within a designated time limit score one point to the team that made them. The teams then change roles. The team with the most points wins.

PADDY'S BLACK PIG

THIS IS GREAT FUN for a small group of children, or for playing one-to-one with a child. The child, or group, is asked questions to which they may only give one answer: 'Paddy's black pig'. Any child who smiles or giggles is out. Carefully framed questions form traps for the unwary: 'Who did you see when you looked in the mirror this morning?' 'Who's your best friend?' 'Who sleeps under your bed?' and so on.

JUMBLED RHYMES

A JUMBLED NURSERY rhyme is needed for each child. You can enlarge and photocopy a rhyme from a book, making as many copies as there will be players, or you can use a different rhyme for each player, making sure they are all the same length or divided into the same number of pieces.

Cut the rhymes into lines, mix up the order of the lines and place the jumbled pieces in an envelope. Each child is given an envelope and when the starting signal is given, players start to sort out their rhymes. The winner is the first player to put the lines of the rhyme in the correct order.

WRONG!

BEFORE THE PARTY, write a short story in which lots of mistakes have been made—for example, in which a character goes to an antique shop to buy a new clock. The children must spot these mistakes as the story is read to them. A child spotting a mistake shouts out 'Wrong!' then has to explain what the mistake is. Each correctly identified mistake scores one point for its spotter. If a child shouts when there is no mistake, he loses a point. The player with the most points at the end of the story wins the game.

PRIZE SUGGESTIONS
A visit to a charity or secondhand shop will prove a worthwhile excursion to prepare for the Hippy Party. At very little cost, you will find all the prizes you need. Look for strings of beads, flower earrings, LP records from the period (it doesn't matter that the record probably won't be able to be played—as long as it has a suitably psychedelic cover, it will be treasured for its novelty value).

INDOOR GAMES

APPLE PARING

GIVE EACH CHILD an apple, a fruit knife and a plate. The apples and knives should be of similar size and quality. The children must carefully peel their apples, the winner being the one to produce the longest and narrowest paring.

BEANBAG HOCKEY

FOR THIS GAME you will need a small beanbag, two chairs and two newspapers, each rolled up tightly and tied with string to form a stick. Divide the children into two teams, and line them up on opposite sides of the room, facing each other. Give each member of one team a number, from left to right, and number the other team with the same numbers from right to left. The teams will then face each other like this:

1	2	3	4	5
5	4	3	2	1

In the centre of the floor, place the newspaper sticks and the beanbag. Place a chair in the centre of each far wall. These will be the goals.

The referee starts play by calling out a number. The two team members with that number run forward, pick up a newspaper stick, and try to hit the beanbag into the goal, that is, between their team's chair legs. Once a goal has been scored, they put back the sticks and the beanbag. The referee can make this a very fast-paced game, by barely giving players a chance to catch their breath. The team with the most goals at the end of the allotted time wins.

CHARADES

DIVIDE THE CHILDREN into teams. Teams write words, phrases, book, movie or television titles for the other team to act out. They write these on a piece of paper and place them in a hat. The team member going first chooses a slip of paper from the opposing team's hat, then has to act out what is written on it for the others to guess. You may wish

to agree on what gestures will be allowed for concepts such as 'sounds like' or how many syllables a word contains, but the only compulsory rule is that the actor cannot speak. Most words will have to be broken up. For example, with the word 'jigsaw' the player could dance a little jig for the first syllable, and pretend to saw some wood for the second. The team members shout out what they think is being depicted until they guess correctly or the time limit expires. More than one person can take part in a charade. With young children it is often better to have at least two, or to pair each child with an adult. You can play the game non-competitively or award prizes for the most imaginative, most energetic or most accurate miming.

PASS THE ORANGE

DIVIDE THE CHILDREN into teams and have them sit down in a line opposite each other. The children place their hands behind their backs. Give the first child in the line an orange to cradle with his feet. At the word 'Go!' the orange must be passed to the feet of the next player, and so on down the line. If the orange drops to the floor it must be returned to the beginning of the line. The first team to pass the orange all the way down the line wins.

THE CHOCOLATE GAME

PLACE A HAT, a scarf, a pair of gloves, a knife, a fork, a plate and a bar of chocolate on the floor in the centre of the room. Sit the children in a circle around these items. The children take turns throwing a die. When one of them throws a six, she has until the next player throws a six to put on the clothing, unwrap the chocolate bar (with gloves on) and eat it with a knife and fork. As soon as another child throws a six she rushes into the circle, removes the hat, scarf and gloves from the first child, puts them on and continues to try to eat the chocolate. The first player goes back to the circle. The game continues until all the chocolate has been eaten.

FISHING COMPETITION

MAKE AN ASSORTMENT of coloured fish from light cardboard. Attach a metal safety pin to the nose of each fish. Write a number on the back of each fish to indicate its weight and arrange the fish in a large shallow dish (which represents the lake) so that the numbers cannot be seen. Give each player a fishing rod, made by tying a small magnet to the end of a pencil with a piece of cotton. The children must try to catch as many fish as possible within a time limit. When all the fish have been caught, everyone adds up the total weight of the fish they have caught.

FLYING FISH

CUT FISH SHAPES, about 25 cm long, from stiff paper or light cardboard. (The cardboard should not be too heavy, or the fish won't fly.) Give a fish to each child, along with a rolled-up magazine or newspaper. Put a line of plates at the opposite end of the room. On their hands and knees, the children must fan their fish with the magazine so that it eventually flutters across the room and lands on a plate. The first child to put a fish on a plate wins.

MYSTERY MATCHBOXES

FILL EIGHT MATCHBOXES with two or three of the same small things, such as dried peas, gravel, sugar, feathers, drawing pins, matches, rice and paperclips. Place a list of the contents on the wall where the children can see it. Pass around each box in turn and ask the children to shake the box and write down what they think is in it. (Make sure you keep track of the order the boxes go around in.) The child with the most correct guesses wins the game.

HAPPY TRAVELLERS

TAKE A SECTION of a newspaper—the sport or fashion pages, for example—and rearrange them by putting them in the wrong order, putting some pages in upside-down, folding some pages inside others, and so on. Children sit facing each other in two rows. They should sit very close together like passengers on a crowded train. Each child is given one of the newspapers, and at the word 'Go!' tries to rearrange the pages of the newspaper into the correct order. The first player to do so wins the game.

HAT MAKING

THIS IS A QUIET game for a small number of children and works very well when played in pairs. Give each pair one newspaper, three sheets of coloured paper, twelve pins, a wad of Blu-tack, a roll of sticky tape and a pair of scissors. The pairs are asked to produce a fancy hat in fifteen minutes, using only the given material. The winning hat is the one voted best by all the players. This game can also be played non-competitively and children can wear their hats throughout the party if they like.

HAT AND SCARF

PROVIDE A HAT, a scarf, a coat and a pair of gloves for each team. Teams line up behind their leaders. Place the clothes on a chair in front of each team. At the starting signal, the leader runs to the chair, puts on the clothes and runs around her team. She then takes off the clothes and gives them to the next player to put on. Play continues in this way down the line. When the last player has run around her team, she places the clothes on the chair. The first team with its set of clothes back on the chair wins the game.

HEDGEHOGS

GIVE EACH CHILD a fairly large potato, a saucer of pins and a pair of gloves. The child puts on the gloves, picks up the pins one at a time and sticks them in the potato. The one who has given the hedgehog the most spines in three minutes is the winner. This is a good game for small parties.

LAUGHING **HANDKERCHIEF**

ONE CHILD IS the leader. The others stand around her in a circle. The leader has a handkerchief, which she drops as a signal for the other players to laugh. They must start laughing as soon as she lets go of the handkerchief and stop when it touches the floor. A player is out if she does not laugh the whole of the time that the handkerchief is falling, or if she continues laughing after it has landed. (The leader may laugh as much as she likes!) The last player left in the game wins.

NECKLACE **RACE**

DIVIDE THE CHILDREN into pairs and line them up at one end of the room. At the opposite end, place one saucer for each pair; in each saucer is twelve beads. Give one child in each pair a needle and a length of heavy thread. At the signal to start the child with needle and thread must thread the needle and tie a large firm knot at one end of the thread. At the same time, the partner runs to the saucer, picks up two beads only, and runs back with them. When the first child has threaded the needle, he takes the two beads and threads them while his partner goes back to the saucer for two more beads. Play continues in this way until all the beads have been threaded. If any beads are dropped they must be picked up and threaded again.

When a child has threaded all twelve beads, he removes the needle and ties the bead necklace around his partner's neck. The game is won by the first pair to finish and put on its necklace.

NO PAWS **ALLOWED**

PUT A WHOLE APPLE on a paper plate, one for each player. Place the plates on the floor. When all the children are kneeling at a plate, with hands clasped behind their backs, give a starting signal. They must eat the apples without using their hands at all. The first to finish is the winner.
Note: If you are prepared to clean them up afterwards, children will love playing this game eating jelly, even ice-cream or chocolate mousse, without using their hands. Many foods are suitable for this game.

NOSE IN THE **MATCHBOX**

DIVIDE THE CHILDREN into two teams and have them stand in a line very close to each other. Give a matchbox lid to the first child in each row. At the starting signal she lodges it on her nose and passes it onto the next player's nose without using her hands. The matchbox lid must be passed down the line. If a player touches the lid with her hands or drops it, it is returned to the start. The first team to successfully pass the lid to the end of the line wins.

pencil & paper games

When children need settling down, or rain starts falling, or the party organiser needs a break . . .try some of these games.

MAKING WORDS

GIVE THE CHILDREN a reasonably long (but comprehensible) word related to the party's theme. For the Dinosaur Party you could choose Brontosaurus, for the Halloween party, Frankenstein, and so on. Children write the word at the top of a sheet of paper and are given ten minutes to make up as many words as they can from the letters. Score by giving a point for each word. If you like, add restrictions to the list such as: words must contain at least four letters, or plurals made by adding an 's' are not counted.

SURPRISE **SENTENCES**

THE OBJECT OF this game is for a team to 'write' a grammatical sentence without planning or conferring. Divide the children into teams. If there are, for example, seven children in a team, they must write a seven-word sentence. Line the teams up in front of a large sheet of paper. Give the first child in line a felt-tip pen. At the signal, the first child runs forward and writes a word on the paper, then runs back and hands the pen to the next child. The next child must write a word before or after the first word then run back to the line. The last child should be able to complete the sentence. If no teams write a sentence, the relay starts again. *Note*: Another version of this game can be played sitting down. The first team member starts a story by writing a few sentences at the top of a large piece of paper. He then folds down the paper, leaving only the last few words exposed; the next team member continues the story and on until the last member of the team who must finish the story. The reading out of these piecemeal stories should prove hilarious. The game can be played non-competitively.

GUESS IN **THE** DARK

GIVE EACH CHILD a pencil and piece of paper. Switch off the lights and pass around a series of objects. (The objects should be commonplace, but perhaps in an unusual form such as a very wrinkled passionfruit or a plastic housefly. Similarly, the objects could be highly textured such as a piece of pumice stone or a bath sponge or have a strong smell, such as an apricot.) When all players have handled them, remove the objects, switch on the lights and ask the children to write down what they think the objects were. The person who correctly lists the most objects is the winner.

TRIVIA QUIZ

PREPARE THIS before the party. You can choose general subjects or limit them to the party theme. Make sure that the questions suit the ability of the children, ranging from questions that are almost too easy to fairly difficult ones. Phrase them so that the answers are short and straightforward, involving the names of characters, players, singers or places, for example. For younger children set up a scoreboard with all the guests' names on it, read out the questions and obtain the answer from the first child whose hand shoots up. Less confident children may form into pairs to help each other. Older children can write down their answers (for added humour you can devise multiple-choice questions), to be scored by an adult at the end of the game. You may want to award first, second and third prizes.

DOTTY DRAWINGS

EACH CHILD has a piece of paper and a pencil and is asked to draw six distinct dots randomly on the page. Once finished, children pass their 'drawings' to the child on the left. Children have to connect the dots to depict a recognisable object. You can nominate these to suit the theme of the party. Aliens would be easy to create, for example, but animals could represent a humorous challenge.

CATEGORIES

A SIMPLE TIME-FILLER for older children is to hand each a piece of paper and pencil and ask them to list as many members of a category that they can think of within a time limit. The more challenging the category the better, for example words ending in the letter 'u' or fruit that must be peeled before eating. The categories can be easily related to the party theme—movies about vampires or types of computers, for example.

PEANUT HUNT

ASK THE CHILDREN to leave the room while you hide ten unshelled peanuts. The peanuts should be at least partly in view. Call the children back, hand them a piece of paper and pencil each and ask them to search the room silently and without touching anything and write down the locations of the peanuts as they find them. The first child to spot all the locations wins.

PRIZE SUGGESTIONS

Handing out the same prize to every winner is a way to avoid arguments, but it can also become predictable. You can still introduce variety, however. For the Snow party, for example, chose a range of 'snow storms' showing different scenes. Give out whistles for the Sports party, but a different type for each winner. As a quieter alternative, make a personalised trophy for each child from plastic goblets and gold or silver inked marker pens.

Action Songs

HERE WE GO ROUND THE MULBERRY BUSH

In this game the children mime the different actions as they sing about them. They dance in a circle and sing:

> *Here we go round the mulberry bush,*
> *the mulberry bush, the mulberry bush,*
> *here we go round the mulberry bush,*
> *on a cold and frosty morning.*

For the next verse they sing and mime:

> *This is the way we wash our clothes,*
> *wash our clothes, wash our clothes,*
> *this is the way we wash our clothes,*
> *on a cold and frosty morning.*

Each child, or an adult, then sings the first line of a new verse and as everyone sings the rest, the actions are mimed. Some suggestions are:

> *This is the way we polish our shoes.*
> *This is the way we wash our hands.*
> *This is the way we clean our teeth.*
> *This is the way we iron our clothes.*
> *This is the way we drink our tea.*
> *This is the way we pat our cat.*
> *This is the way we walk to school.*

Keep the actions familiar and children will probably want to play the game for some time. When they run out of ideas, stop the game and start another.

THE FARMER IN THE DELL

The children choose a farmer (probably the birthday child) and form a circle. They walk around the farmer singing:

> *The farmer's in the dell,*
> *the farmer's in the dell,*
> *hey-ho, the derry-o,*
> *the farmer's in the dell.*

The farmer then chooses a partner to stand inside the circle with him, and the children walk in a circle, singing:

> *The farmer takes a wife,*
> *the farmer takes a wife,*
> *hey-ho, the derry-o,*
> *the farmer takes a wife.*

The verse is then repeated with the following additions:

> *The wife takes a child;*
> *The child takes a nurse;*
> *The nurse takes a dog.*

Each time, the last child nominated chooses another one to step into the circle. Finally, everyone sings:

> *We all pat the dog,*
> *we all pat the dog,*
> *hey-ho, the derry-o,*
> *we all pat the dog.*

As they do this they pat the dog on the back. The game starts all over again, usually with the dog becoming the farmer.

ORANGES AND LEMONS

One player elects to be an orange, the other a lemon. The orange and lemon form an arch by holding hands above their heads. While all sing the following rhyme, the other players file under the arch in a continuous line.

> *'Oranges and lemons,'*
> *say the bells of St Clements.*
> *'You owe me five farthings,'*
> *say the bells of St Martins.*
> *'When will you pay me?'*
> *say the bells of Old Bailey.*
> *'When I grow rich,'*
> *say the bells of Shoreditch.*
> *'When will that be?'*
> *say the bells of Stepney.*
> *'I'm sure I don't know,'*
> *says the great bell of Bow.*

> *Here comes a candle to light you to bed.*
> *Here comes a chopper to chop off your head.*

With the words 'chop off your head', the two children forming the arch capture the child who is walking through the arch at the time. The captured child must stand on the orange side of the arch. The next captured child must stand on the lemon side. The pattern continues until all are captured. Oranges then have a tug of war with the lemons.

RING-A-RING-OF-ROSES

Players form a circle and join hands, then skip around singing:

> *Ring-a-ring-of-roses*
> *A pocketful of posies*
> *A tishoo! A tishoo!*
> *We all fall down.*

At the words 'fall down', they all collapse on the floor. For older children, ring the changes by gradually eliminating the last player to fall down.

PRIZE SUGGESTIONS
Older children, and certainly teenagers, can regard games and prizes as childish, so choose games and prizes that are appropriate to their age-group. Something suggestively 'adult' such as a sheet of temporary tattoos will probably appeal to older children, however, if your guests really don't want to play, don't force them. It will ruin the party.

OUTDOOR GAMES & RACES

APPLE BOBBING

FILL A LARGE basin with water and float apples in it. The children must kneel down next to the basin and attempt to catch apples using only their mouths. The first child to capture an apple and fish it out of the water wins. (This game must be supervised closely.)

BACK-TO-BACK RACE

DIVIDE THE CHILDREN into pairs and have them stand back-to-back, locking their arms at the elbows. The pair must run, as best they can, from one line to another, face the other way and run back again. The first pair to get back to the starting line wins.

BLOWING BUBBLES

THIS CAN be a non-competitive activity for very young children. A supply of plastic bubble pipes and liquid (water mixed with washing-up liquid) can keep them amused for some time. It can be made more interesting by seeing who can blow the biggest bubble, or whose bubble lasts the longest, flies the highest or farthest, and so on.

BRICK RACE

LINE THE CHILDREN up on the starting line and give each child two house bricks. The children must progress to the finishing line by 'walking' on these bricks—balancing on one while picking up the other and moving it forward. (Decide whether anyone who falls off will be forced to go back to the start, disqualified or allowed to continue from that spot.) The first to reach the finish line wins. (This is quite a difficult game, so play it with older, stronger children only.)

CROCODILE RACE

DIVIDE THE CHILDREN into two teams and line them up behind the starting line. The children squat down, one behind the other, to form a 'crocodile'. The crocodiles race to the finishing line in little jumps or bounces. If a child loses contact with the child in front, her team must stop and reassemble. The back end of the crocodile must stay where it is, while the front end moves back to join it. The first team to reach the finish line intact wins the race.

SACK RACE

GIVE EACH CHILD a hessian sack or large pillow case. The children must line up at the starting line and jump to the finish line, holding the sack around himself. The first child to reach the finish line wins.

DOUGHNUT-EATING RACE

HANG SHORT LENGTHS of string from the clothesline, one for each player. Tie a doughnut on the end of each string. (The height of the string should be adjusted to ensure that every child must stand on tiptoe to reach the doughnut with her mouth.) The children stand under their doughnut with hands behind backs, and the first child to finish eating the doughnut wins.

DROP THE HANDKERCHIEF

HAVE THE CHILDREN form a well-spaced circle facing inwards. Whoever opts to be 'it' runs around outside the circle with a handkerchief. At any stage she can drop the handkerchief behind one of the players in the circle. Immediately the player discovering the handkerchief must pick up the handkerchief and chase the 'it' around the circle. If 'it' beats the child back to the vacated space, she joins the

circle. The child outside the circle takes a turn dropping the handkerchief. (The children can sing a song while in the circle, often 'A Tisket, A Tasket'.)

DUCKLING RACE

THIS IS A straight race from a starting to a finishing line, but children are hampered by having to waddle along in a crouched position, with their 'wings' flapping— that is, their hands tucked into their armpits and their elbows waggling. Any duckling losing its balance must get back into a crouch before moving on.

EGG AND SPOON RACE

GIVE EVERY CHILD a hard-boiled egg and a spoon. She must hold the egg, balanced on the spoon, while running from the start line to the finish line. To make this game more complicated for older children, make a rule that if they drop their egg they must put it back on the spoon, go back to the

start line and begin again. A variation of this race can be played with each runner holding two spoons, containing an egg each. Small potatoes could be substituted for hard-boiled eggs.

FOLLOW THE LEADER

WITH MUSIC PLAYING, an adult leads a line of children around the house or garden, skipping, hopping, jogging and performing odd actions which the children copy. Crawl under tables, jump over benches and skip in and out of trees. The more varied, the better.

HOT POTATO RELAY

DIVIDE THE CHILDREN into two teams. Give both teams a spoon and a basket. Make two rows of potatoes in front of each team. They should be very well spaced and there should be the same number of potatoes as there are

team members. On the starting signal, the first player runs to the first potato, picks it up with the spoon (not hands), and carries it back to drop in the basket at the starting line. She then gives the spoon to the next player, who runs, picks up the next potato and brings it back to the basket. The first team to get all the potatoes into the basket wins the game.

OVERPASS, UNDERPASS

DIVIDE THE CHILDREN into teams and have each form a line. Team members must pass a selection of objects—a set of stuffed animals or a variety of differently sized balls— via their upraised hands from the first player to the last in the line. When the object reaches the last player, he returns the objects back between the legs of the players until it reaches the front. For extra fun and confusion, do not wait for one object to return to the front of the line before sending the next on its way. The object of the game is to get all the objects back to the beginning of the line as fast as possible.

PIGGYBACK JOUSTING

PLAY THIS GAME on grass or a large clear, carpeted area. Children pair off and decide who will take first turn at being the 'mount' and who will be the 'rider'. Two pairs at a time ride towards each other and the riders attempt to dislodge each other from their 'mounts'. If any part of the rider touches the ground, the rider is held to have been dislodged. Before each joust, pairs must decide whether the mounts will run upright or go on all fours (which is slower, but not so far to fall). Losing pairs may take another turn with their roles reversed.

Keep track of all results and play off winning pairs against each other until the tournament is won.

TORTOISE RACE

BICYCLES CAN BE used for this slow-motion race, or the children can crawl, hop, skip or simply walk. Set a start and finish line. The slowest person in this race is the winner. The children must be spaced well apart if they are using bikes, so as not to wobble into each other. At the word 'Go!' the children must move in as straight a line as possible towards the finish line, and keep moving, as slowly as possible without stopping. The last rider/racer to reach the finishing line is the winner.

TEDDYBACK RACE

CHILDREN LINE UP on all fours at one end of the course. Place a teddy bear on each child's back. This must be carried to the finish line without falling off. If a teddy falls, its owner must pick it up, return to the start line, and begin again. The first child to successfully complete the course is the winner.

THREE-LEGGED RACE

DIVIDE THE CHILDREN into pairs. Use a scarf or large handkerchief to tie the right leg of one person to the left leg of the other. The pair must race as one three-legged person from start to finish line. (A little practice period should be allowed before this race.)

TUG OF WAR

YOU WILL NEED a strong rope, at least four metres long. Divide the players into two teams. The sturdiest person of each team is to be the 'anchor' at each end of the rope. Draw a line on the ground between the two teams. The team that succeeds in pulling the other over the line wins.

WATER RACE

DIVIDE THE CHILDREN into teams and have each team form a line. At the head of each line is an empty bucket, with a larger bucket full of water some distance away. Give the first member of each team a plastic mug. Using this, the team must transfer water from the full bucket to the empty one, by running in turn to the full bucket and bringing back a mug of water. The first team to fill their bucket wins.
Note: For extra fun, you could add some soap suds to the water. The children will probably get quite wet during this game so have some towels standing by.

Games OF Trickery & Surprise

THE CAPTAIN'S COMING

NOMINATE ONE side of the room to be port, and another to be starboard. Also nominate places or pieces of furniture to be a rowboat, the anchor, the main mast, the cannon and so on. All children form a group in the centre of the room. Call

out the key phrase and add a command, for example, 'The Captain's coming—run to starboard!' or 'The Captain's coming—scrub the decks!' The last person to obey the command is out. Other commands could be to salute, to run to the rowboat, to lift the anchor, and so on. The last sailor left to command is the winner.

FROGGY, FROGGY, MAY WE CROSS YOUR SHINING RIVER?

ONE CHILD IS elected to be Froggy, and stands with her back to the rest of the group. Mark two parallel lines, with a good space—about 4–5 metres—between them. Froggy stands behind the line on one side, and the rest of the group stands behind the line on the other side.

Together the group chants, 'Froggy, Froggy, may we cross your shining river?' Froggy responds, 'Not unless you wear the colour . . . blue!' or, 'Not unless you wear . . .green socks!' or whatever Froggy chooses. At the key word or phrase Froggy turns quickly to face the rest of the group, and the child or children wearing the nominated colour or clothing must race across the river without being caught by Froggy. The child who is caught becomes the next Froggy, and the last frog returns to the group.

GRANDMOTHER'S FOOTSTEPS

ONE CHILD is 'Grandmother'. All the other children stand in line some distance away. Grandmother stands with her back to the children; the children must creep forward towards her. Whenever Grandmother quickly turns around, they must stand still. If she sees any of them moving, they must return to the starting line again. The first to reach Grandmother becomes the next Grandmother.

BIRDS FLY

THIS A GAME for very young children. Sit the children on the floor with both hands on the ground. Their hands must stay there unless the leader (an adult) mentions something that flies. If the leader says 'pigeons fly', the children must raise their hands, but if it is something that does not fly (eggs or giraffes, for example) their hands must stay down. Children who make a mistake are disqualified until only the winner is left.

SIMON SAYS

ALSO KNOWN AS 'O'Grady Says'. The children face Simon, who performs various actions and gives an instruction that begins with 'Simon says'. 'Touch your toes', for example. Some instructions deliberately omit the phrase, for example, 'Simon says touch your toes' and then 'Hold your nose'. The children must only follow instructions which begin with 'Simon says'. Players who make a mistake are out. The last child remaining is the winner.

ON THE BANK, IN THE RIVER

LINE THE CHILDREN up behind a marked line. The side they are standing on is the bank; the other side is the river. Call out 'In the river!' or 'On the bank!', mixing up the commands. Children have to jump to the correct side. Those who do not are out.

WHAT'S THE TIME, MR WOLF?

CHOOSE ONE CHILD to be the wolf. A den or safe place is chosen at the start. The wolf prowls around followed by the rest of the children, who keep calling, 'What's the time, Mr Wolf?' The wolf must answer with a time of the day—one o'clock, six o'clock, half-past four and so on. When the wolf, at his discretion, growls 'Dinner time!' the children must dash for the den. If the wolf catches

anyone before they reach the safe area, the victim becomes the next wolf. Alternatively, this game can be played by elimination—each child caught sits down, and the last player to be caught becomes the wolf for the next round.

WOBBLING BUNNIES

PLAYERS MAKE THEIR hands into ears at the sides of their heads and bunny-hop about, pretending to be rabbits. At the call of 'Danger!' they freeze, and must keep absolutely still for the count of five. Any player who moves so much as a whisker during the count is out.

THE BOILER BURST!

SIT THE CHILDREN down and start telling them a story— the sillier the better. Explain to them that when you use the phrase 'and then the boiler burst!' they must get up and run to a prearranged spot. The story can be as brief or as drawn-out as you like but it should be full of false climaxes, so that by the time you use the phrase 'and then the boiler burst!' the children, themselves, are almost ready to burst with anticipation. The first child to reach the designated spot is the winner.

TEMPLATES

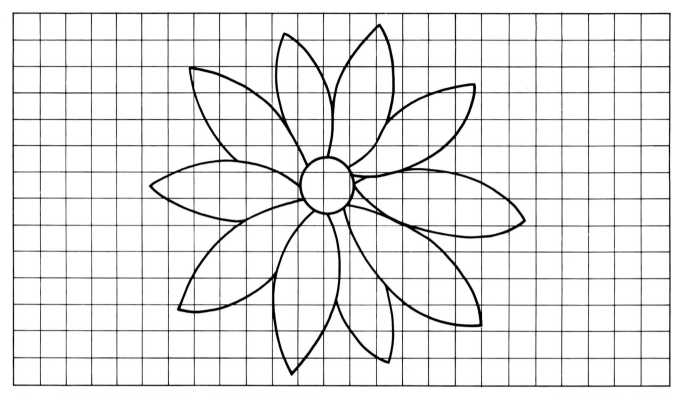

Above: FLOWER POWER Below: JACK-O'-LANTERN   1 SQUARE = 17MM

Use the diagrams in this chapter to make templates for the theme-related shape cakes on pages 20–37. You can copy the drawings onto graph paper or enlarge on a photocopier (try the local library or newsagent) to the desired size.

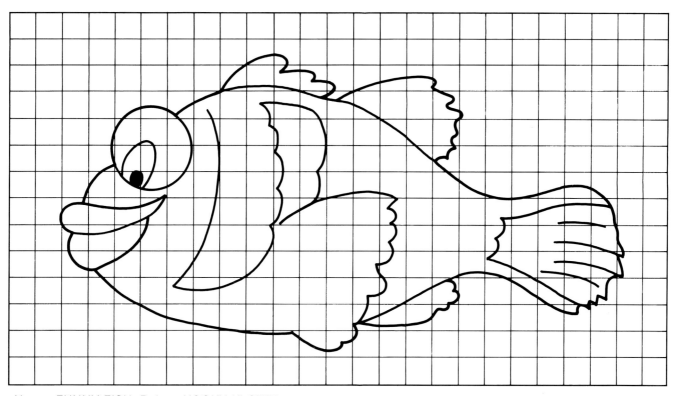

Above: FUNNY FISH Below: KOOKY KLOWN   1 SQUARE = 17MM

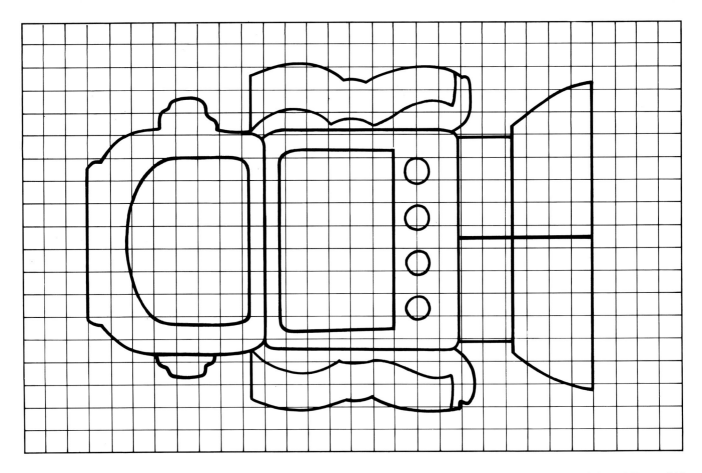

Above: ROBBIE THE ROBOT Below: LOOPY LION   1 SQUARE = 2 CM

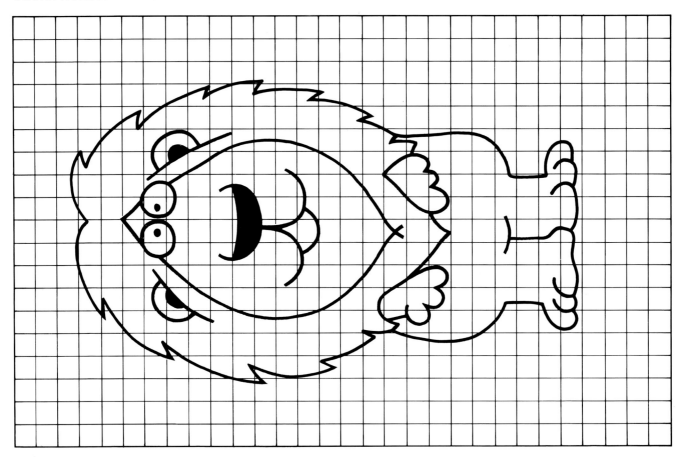

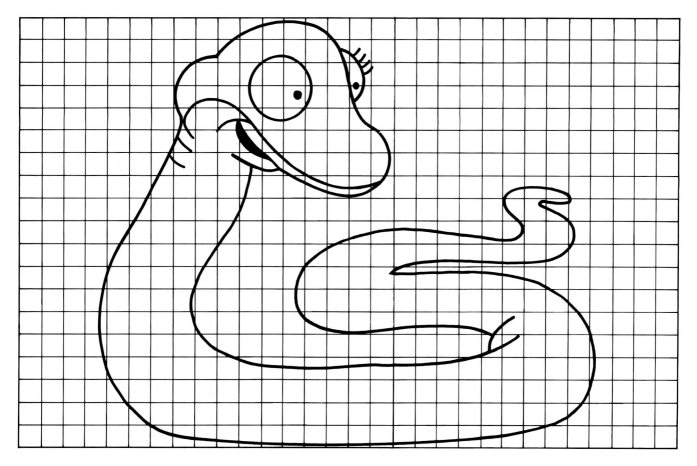

Above: SNAKE CAKE Below: TOM TEDDY

1 SQUARE = 2 CM

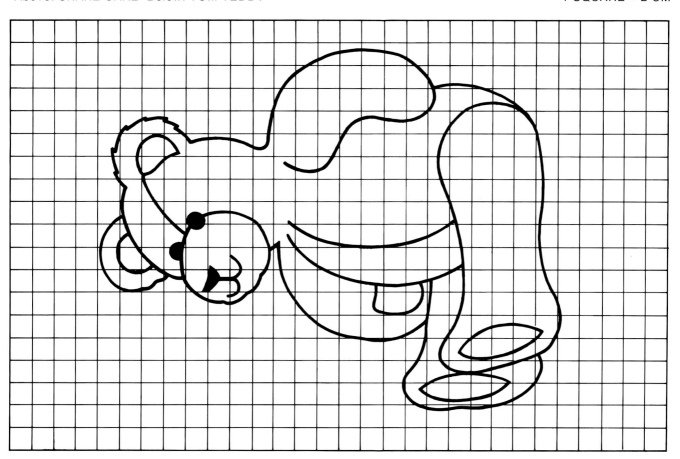

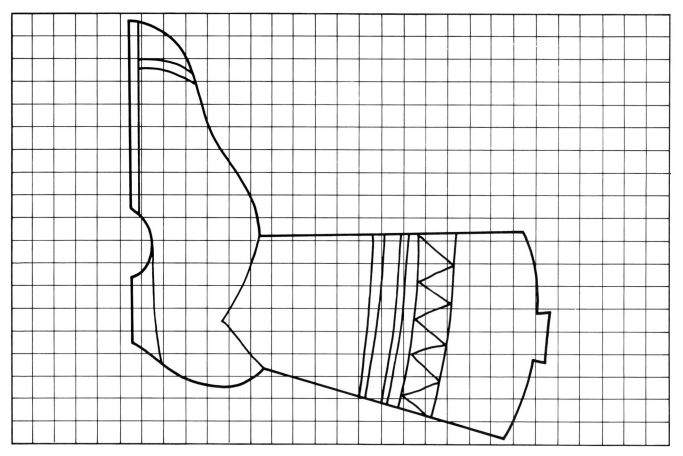

Above: TEXAS BOOT Below: PRETTY STAR   1 SQUARE = 2 CM

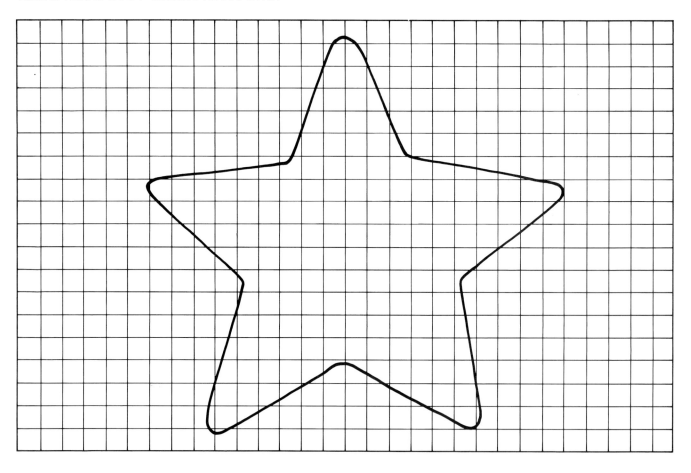

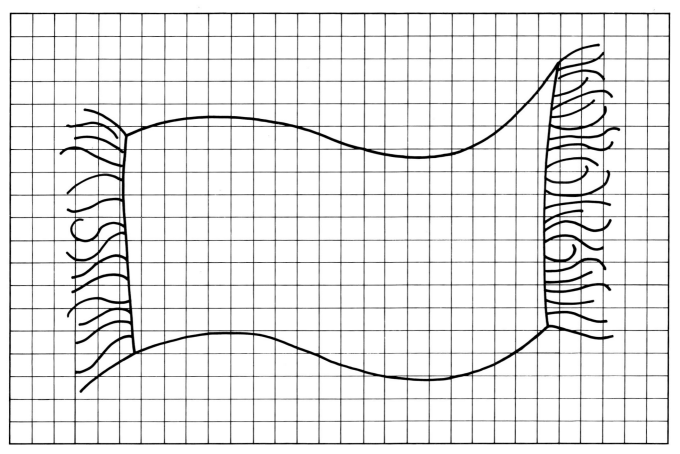

Above: MAGIC CARPET Below: SPACESHIP   1 SQUARE = 2 CM

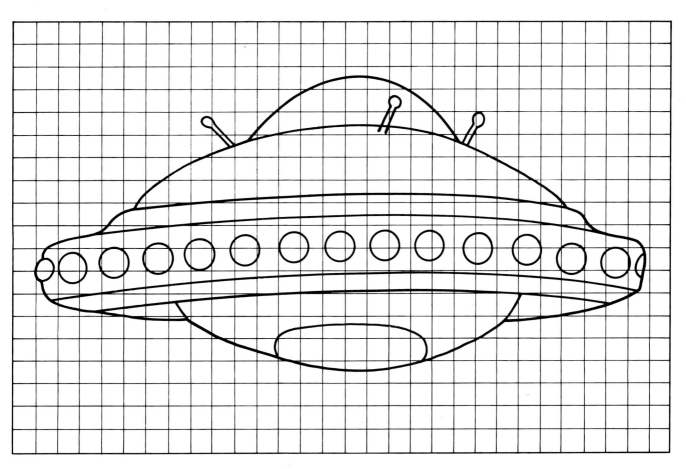

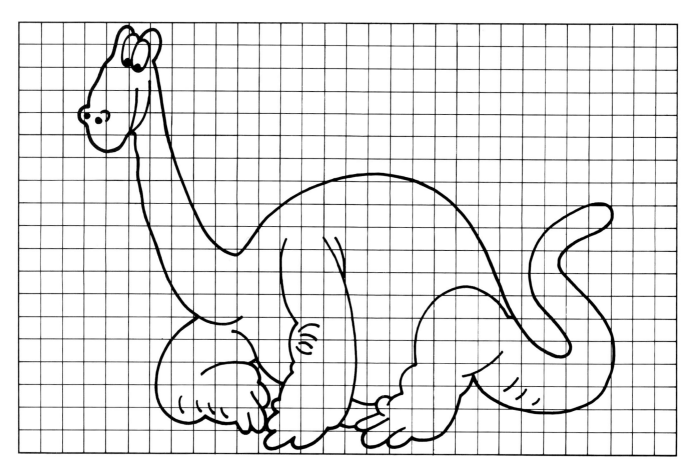

Above: DINO THE DINOSAUR Below: TREASURE CHEST   1 SQUARE = 2 CM

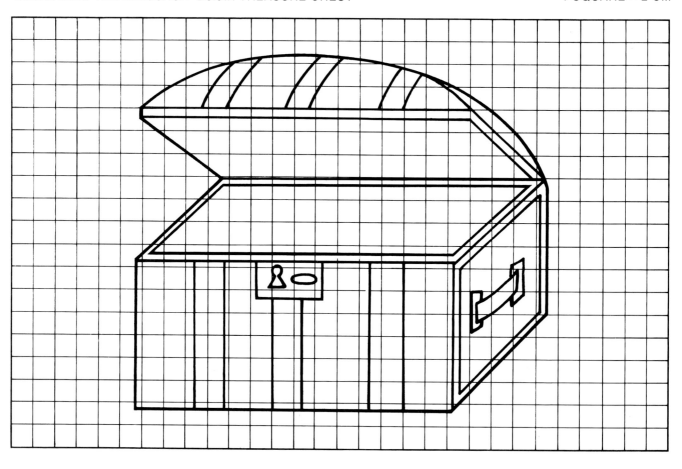

Above: SUNSHINE CAKE Below: PETE THE PENGUIN   1 SQUARE = 2 CM

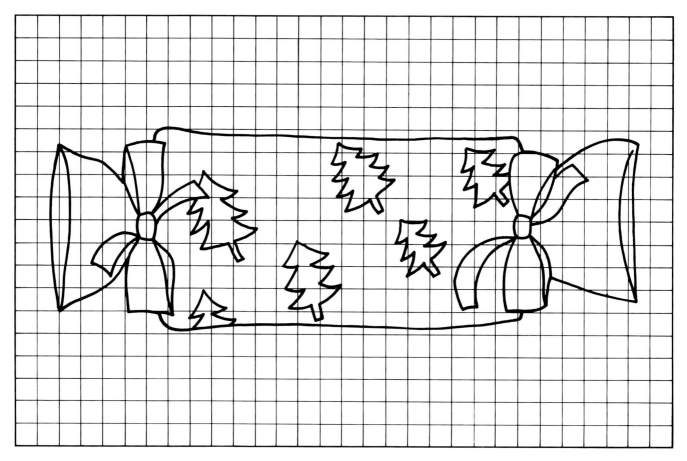

Above: CHRISTMAS CRACKER Below: PUNK HEAD

1 SQUARE = 2 CM

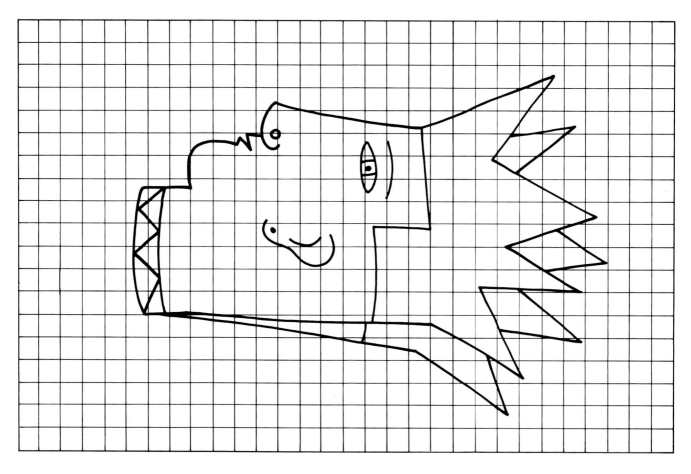

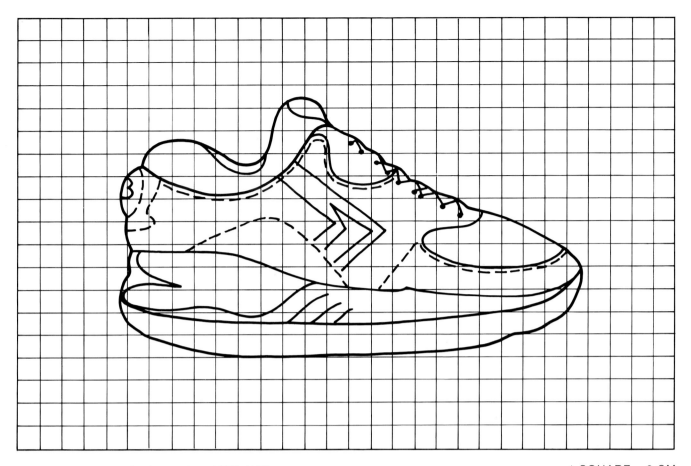

Above: RUNNING SHOE Below: THE AMP   1 SQUARE = 2 CM

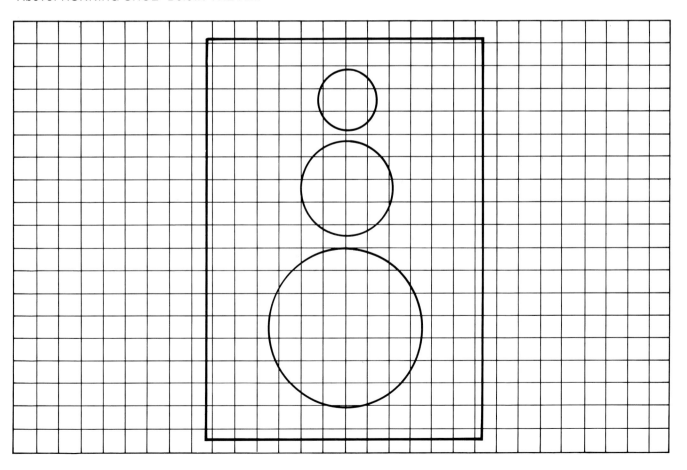

INDEX

A

American Hot Dogs, 65
Amp Cake, The, 37
    Template, 109
Animal Crisps, 50
Animal Feed, 51
Animalia Game, 84
Ant Cordial, 68
Apple Bobbing Game, 96
Apple Paring Game, 90
Arabian Nights Theme, 12
    Take-home Treats, 74

B

Baby Burgers, 45
Back-to-back Race, 96
Balloon, Bat the, 80
Balloon Fight, 80
Balloon Hop, 80
Balloon Volleyball, 80
Balloons, Whizzing, 81
Banana, Nut and Date
    Fingers, 49
Banana Bites, Frozen, 44
Banana Buns, Sticky, 63
Banana Yoghurt Smoothie,
    69
Basic Buttercake, 18
Basic Buttercream, 18, 19
Bat the Balloon, 80
Beach Baby Jellies, 54
Beach Theme, 10
    Take-home Treats, 72
Beanbag Hockey, 90
Birds Fly Game, 99
Biscuits
    Martian, 47
    Pirate Face, 46–7
    Punk Faces, 46–7
    Stained Glass, 64
Bleeding Fingers, 58
Blindfold Drawing, 84
Blindman's Buff, 85
Blood Baths, 58
Blowing Bubbles, 96
Boiler Burst Game, The, 99
Brick Race, 96
Broomstick Relay, 81
Brownies
    Crunchy Top, 54
    Frosted, 54
Bugs in Rugs, 60

Burgers, 45, 52
Buttercake, Basic, 18
Buttercream, Basic, 18,19

C

Cactus Juice, 67
Camel Humps, 49
Captain's Coming Game,
    The, 98
Captives Game, 83
Caramel Popcorn Balls, 59
Carrot Cake, 41
Categories Game, 93
Cavemen Clubs, 44
Charades, 90
Cheeky Face Pikelets, 57
Cheese and Bacon Tarts, 43
Cheese and Salmon Tarts, 43
Cheese Row Boats, Corny, 46
Cheese Scrolls, Ham and, 62
Cheese Swags, 61
Cherry Crunch, 59
Chicken Nuggets, 50
Chicken Toasts, 43
Choc-cherry Spiders, 62
Choc-chip Crackles, 49
Choc-chip Fudge, 64
Choc-coated Iceblocks, 65
Choc-mint Cone Cakes, 62
Chocolate Float Drink, 68
Chocolate Game, The, 90
Chocolate Haystacks, 51
Christmas Cracker Cake, 35
    Template, 108
Christmas Theme, 14
    Take-home Treats, 76
Circus Theme, 16
    Take-home Treats, 78
Clown Faces, 58
Coconut Ice, 55
Cola Spider Drink, 67
Cool Breeze Drink, 67
Cordial, Ant, 68
Corn Cobs with Butter, 56
Corny Cheese Row Boats, 46
Crocodile Race, 96
Crunchy Top Brownies, 54

D

Desert Sand, 49
Dino the Dinosaur Cake, 22
    Template, 106

Dinosaur Eggs, 45
Dinosaurs Theme, 9
    Take-home Treats, 71
Dip, Onion, 61
Disco Theme, 17
    Take-home Treats, 79
Doll Cake, 39
Dotty Drawings, 93
Drop the Handkerchief
    Game, 97
Doughnut-eating Race, 97
Duckling Race, 97

E

Egg and Spoon Race, 97

F

Fairies Theme, 8
    Take-home Treats, 70
Fairy Bread, Psychedelic,
    42
Fairy Cakes, 42
Fairy (Age) Cake, 41
Fairy Wands, 42
Fancy Dress, Planning, 6
Farmer in the Dell Game,
    The, 94
Fish Cocktails, 52
Fishermen's Burgers,
    52
Fishing Competition, 91
Flower Power Cake, 31
    Template, 100
Fluffy Icing, 18, 19
Flying Fish Game, 91
Foaming Craters Drink,
    66
Follow the Leader, 97
Food and Drink, Planning,
    6–7
Frankfurt Bonbons, 59
Froggy, Froggy, May We
    Cross Your Shining
    River? Game, 98
Frosted Brownies, 54
Frozen Banana Bites, 44
Frozen Goo, 57
Fruit Jelly Shapes, 51
Fruit Punch, 67
Fudge, Choc-chip, 64
Funny Fish Cake, 36
    Template, 101

G

Galactic Discs, 47
Games, Planning, 7
Gods and Goddesses Game,
    86
Grand Chain Game, 87
Grandmother's Footsteps
    Game, 99
Great Outdoors Theme, The,
    13
    Take-home Treats, 75
Guacamole and Corn Chips,
    56
Guess in the Dark Game,
    92–3
Guess What Game, 85

H

Halloween Theme, 12
    Take-home Treats, 74
Ham and Cheese Scrolls, 62
Ham and Egg Roll, 65
Ham and Pineapple
    Pinwheels, 54
Happy Travellers Game, 91
Hat and Scarf Game, 91
Hat Making Game, 91
Hedgehogs Game, 91
Here We Go Round the
    Mulberry Bush Game, 94
High Steppers Game, 86
Hippies Theme, 13
    Take-home Treats, 75
Hop and Pop Game, 81
Hot Bean Dogs, 65
Hot Dog Boats, 65
Hot Dogs
    American, 65
    Bean, 65
Hot Potato Game, 86
Hot Potato Relay, 97

I

I Asked the Genie of the
    Lamp Game, 88
I Went to Mars Game, 88
Iceblocks, Choc-coated, 65
Ice-cream Cones, Meteor,
    48–9
Icing, Fluffy, 18, 19
Insy Winsy Spiders, 60
Invitations, 5–6

J

Jack-o'-Lantern Cake, 26
    Template, 100
Jellies, Beach Baby, 54
Jelly Shapes, Fruit, 51
Jumbled Rhymes, 89
Jump the Broom Game 86
Jungle Juice, 66

K

Kids' Style Nachos, 56
Kooky Klown Cake, 34
    Template, 101

L

Laughing Handkerchief
    Game, 92
Lemon Thirst Drink, 69
Lifesavers, 52
Limbo Game, 86
Loopy Lion Cake, 24
    Template, 102

M

Maggot Mounds, 62
Magic Carpet Cake, 27
    Template, 104
Magpies Game, 82
Making Words Game, 92
Malted Milkshake, 69
Mango Wizz Drink, 69
Martian Biscuits, 47
Meatballs, 45
Memory Test, 88
Meteor Ice-cream Cones,
    48–9
Milkshake, Malted, 69
Mini Pizzas, 50
Mismatches Game, 88
Moo Juice, 66
Moon Moguls, 46
Motor Oil Drink, 67
Mouse Traps, 57
Muesli Bars, Toffee, 65
Musical Blackout, 86
Musical Bumps, 86
Musical Chairs, 86
Musical Hats, 87
Musical Hotch Potch, 87
Musical Islands, 87
Musical Magic Carpet, 87
Musical Sets, 88
Musical Statues, 87
Musical Torch, 88
Mystery Matchboxes, 91
Mystery Parcel, 88

N

Nachos, Kids' Style, 56
Necklace Race, 92
No Paws Allowed Game, 92
Nose in the Matchbox, 92

O

On the Bank, in the River
    Game, 99
Onion Dip, 61
Oranges and Lemons Game,
    95
Outdoors Theme, The Great,
    13
    Take-home Treats, 75
Outer Space Theme, 8
    Take-home Treats, 70
Overpass, Underpass Game,
    97

P

Paddy's Black Pig Game, 89
Palm Tree Cake, 39
Partners Game, 82
Pass the Orange, 90
Pass the Parcel, 88
Peach Dream Drink, 68
Peanut Hunt, 93
Pete the Penguin Cake, 23
    Template, 107
Piggyback Jousting, 98
Pikelets,
    Cheeky Face, 57
    Scary Face, 57
Pin the Tail on the Camel, 84
Pin the Tail on the Donkey,
    84
Pin the Tail on the Rat, 84
Pin the Tail on the
    Triceratops, 84
Pineapple Cream Crush
    Drink, 67
Pineapple Pinwheels, Ham
    and, 54
Pirate Face Biscuits, 46–7
Pirates Theme, 9
    Take-home Treats, 71
Pizza, 64
Pizzas, Mini, 50
Planning Kids' Parties, 4–5
Poison Potion Drink, 66
Popcorn Balls, Caramel, 59
Popcorn Pearls, 53
Postman's Holiday Game, 82
Postman's Island Holiday
    Game, 82
Potato Wedges, 56
Prawn Toasts, 43
Present Hunt, 82
Pretty Star Cake, 18
    Template, 105
Prizes
    Planning, 7
    Suggestions for, 85, 87, 89,
        93, 95
    See also Individual
        Themes
Psychedelic Fairy Bread, 42

Punch, Fruit, 67
Punk Cake, 33
    Template, 108
Punk Faces Biscuits, 46–7
Punk Theme, 15
    Take-home Treats, 77

R

Reflexes Game, 88
Ring Game, The, 83
Ring-a-ring-of-roses Game,
    95
Robbie the Robot Cake, 25
    Template, 102
Robots and Computers
Theme, 11
    Take-home Treats, 73
Rock Cakes, 48
Rocky Road, 44
Rudolph's Punch, 68
Running Shoe Cake, 31
    Template, 109

S

Sack Race, 96
Sandwiches, Zebra, 50
Sardines Game, 83
Sausage Rolls, 46
Sausage Sizzle, 61
Scary Face Pikelets, 57
Scavenger Hunt, 82
Sea Cake, 37
Simon Says, 99
Skateboarder Cake, 38
Small Toffees, 60
Smoothie, Banana Yoghurt,
    69
Snake Cake, 28
    Template, 103
Snake (Age) Cake, 36
Snow Theme, 10
    Take-home Treats, 72
Snowmen, 55
Soldier Cake, 36
Space Ship Cake, 19
    Template, 104
Space Spuds, 47
Speckled Bubble Bars, 53
Spider Drink, Cola, 67
Sport Theme, 16
    Take-home Treats, 78
Squeak, Piggy, Squeak!
    Game, 85
Squelch and Crunch, 58
Stained Glass Biscuits, 64
Star Cake, Pretty, 18
    Template, 105
Star Dust, 49
Starry Night Crisps, 50
Sticky Banana Buns, 63
String Hunt, 83
Sunburst Parfait, 53

Sunken Subs, 52
Sunshine Cake, 22
    Template, 107
Surprise Sentences, 92
Swamp Mud, 44

T

Take-home Treats, Planning,
    7
Tarts
    Cheese and Bacon, 43
    Cheese and Salmon, 43
Teddy Bear Cakes, 63
Teddy Bears Picnic Theme,
    14
    Take-home Treats, 76
Teddyback Race, 98
Texas Boot Cake, 32
    Template, 105
Themes, Planning, 6
Thieves Game, 85
Three-legged Race, 98
Toadstools, 48
Toasts
    Chicken, 43
    Prawn, 43
Toffee Muesli Bars, 65
Toffees, Small, 60
Tom Teddy Cake, 30
    Template, 103
Tortoise Race, 98
Train Cake, 38
Treasure Chest Cake, 21
    Template, 106
Treasure Hunt, 83
Trivia Quiz, 93
Tug of War, 98

U

UFOs, 48
Underwater Theme, 17
    Take-home Treats, 79

W

Water Race, 98
What's the Time, Mr Wolf?
Game, 99
White Christmas, 63
Whizzing Balloons, 81
Wild West Theme, 15
    Take-home Treats, 77
Wild West Wind Game,
    81
Witches' Brew Drink, 67
Wobbling Bunnies Game,
    99
Wrong! Game, 89

Z

Zebra Sandwiches, 50
Zoo Theme, 11
    Take-home Treats, 73

1 cm
2 cm
3 cm
4 cm
5 cm
6 cm
7 cm
8 cm
9 cm
10 cm
11 cm
12 cm
13 cm
14 cm
15 cm
16 cm
17 cm
18 cm
19 cm
20 cm
21 cm
22 cm
23 cm
24 cm
25 cm

USEFUL INFORMATION

All our recipes are thoroughly tested in the Family Circle® Test Kitchen. Standard metric measuring cups and spoons approved by Standards Australia are used in the development of our recipes. All cup and spoon measurements are level. We have used 60 g eggs in all recipes. Sizes of cans vary from manufacturer to manufacturer and between countries—use the can size closest to the one suggested in the recipes.

Conversion Guide		
1 cup = 250 ml (8 fl oz)		
1 teaspoon = 5 ml		
1 Australian tablespoon = 20 ml (4 teaspoons)		
1 UK/US tablespoon = 15 ml (3 teaspoons)		

Dry Measures	Liquid Measures	Linear Measures
30 g = 1 oz	30 ml = 1 fl oz	6 mm = $\frac{1}{4}$ inch
250 g = 8 oz	125 ml = 4 fl oz	1 cm = $\frac{1}{2}$ inch
500 g = 1 lb	250 ml = 8 fl oz	2.5 cm = 1 inch

Oven Temperatures		
Electric	°C	°F
Very slow	120	250
Slow	150	300
Mod slow	160	325
Moderate	180	350
Mod hot	210	425
Hot	240	475
Very hot	260	525
Gas	°C	°F
Very slow	120	250
Slow	150	300
Mod slow	160	325
Moderate	180	350
Mod hot	190	375
Hot	200	400
Very hot	230	450

Cup Conversions—Dry Ingredients

1 cup breadcrumbs, dry = 125 g (4 oz)

    soft = 60 g (2 oz)

1 cup caster sugar = 220 g (7 oz)

1 cup cheese, grated, lightly packed:

    natural cheddar = 125 g (4 oz)

    processed cheddar = 155 g (5 oz)

1 cup cherries, glacé, chopped, whole = 185 g (5 oz)

1 cup flour, plain or self-raising = 125 g (4 oz)

1 cup sugar, caster = 220 g (7 oz)

International Glossary

biscuit	cookie
chips	crisps
silver balls	dragees
sultana	raisin

Published by Murdoch Books®, a division of Murdoch Magazines Pty Limited, 213 Miller Street, North Sydney NSW 2060.

Murdoch Books® Food Editor: Kerrie Ray. **Assistant Food Editor:** Tracy Rutherford. **Family Circle® Food Editor:** Jo Anne Calabria. **Editor:** Amanda Bishop. **Designer:** Marylouise Brammer. **Author:** Margo Lanagan
Recipe Development: Maria Sampsonis. Cakes Concepts and Development: (Number Cakes) Michelle Withers, (Theme Cakes) Kerrie Ray. **Photography:** (Food, Drinks and Cover) Jon Bader, (Take-home Treats, End Papers and Theme Cakes) Sue Stubbs. (Number Cakes) Joe Filshie. **Photographer's Assistant:** (Take-home Treats) Paula Pellegrini.
Additional Photography: (Cover) Luis Martin. **Food Styling:** (Food, Drinks and Cover) Carolyn Fienberg (Cakes) Kerrie Ray. **Food Preparation:** Ann Bollard, Jo Forrest, Wendy Goggin, Maria Sampsonis, Chris Sheppard.

Illustrations: page 8 (top), 10 (top), 12 (top), 14 (top), 16 (top) 80–99 Louise Pfanner, page 8 (bottom),10 (bottom), 12 (bottom), 14 (bottom), 16 (bottom) Dawn Tyack, page 9 (top), 11 (top), 13 (top), 15 (top), 17 (top) John Yates, page 9 (bottom), 11 (bottom), 13 (bottom), 15 (bottom), 17 (bottom) Skye Rogers (Templates and Number Cake Diagrams) Jayne Hunter.
Publisher: Anne Wilson. **Publishing Manager:** Catie Ziller. **Production Coordinator:** Liz Fitzgerald. **Managing Editor:** Susan Tomnay. **Studio Manager:** Norman Baptista. **International Manager:** Mark Newman. **Marketing Manager:** Mark Smith. **National Sales Manager:** Keith Watson. **Key Accounts Sales Manager:** Kim Deacon. **Photo Librarian:** Dianne Bedford.
National Library of Australia Cataloguing-in-Publication Data. Kids Party Book. Includes index. ISBN 0 86411 388 9. 1. Cookery. 2. Children's parties. 641.568. Printed by Prestige Litho, Queensland.